T0380793

Certification Study Companion Series

The Apress Certification Study Companion Series offers guidance and hands-on practice to support technical and business professionals who are studying for an exam in the pursuit of an industry certification. Professionals worldwide seek to achieve certifications in order to advance in a career role, reinforce knowledge in a specific discipline, or to apply for or change jobs. This series focuses on the most widely taken certification exams in a given field. It is designed to be user friendly, tracking to topics as they appear in a given exam and work alongside other certification material as professionals prepare for their exam.

More information about this series at https://link.springer.com/bookseries/17100.

Salesforce Platform App Builder Certification Companion

Mastering the Essentials for Exam Success and Beyond

Second Edition

Rakesh Gupta

Apress®

Salesforce Platform App Builder Certification Companion: Mastering the Essentials for Exam Success and Beyond, Second Edition

Rakesh Gupta
Dallas, Texas, USA

ISBN-13 (pbk): 979-8-8688-1272-9   ISBN-13 (electronic): 979-8-8688-1273-6
https://doi.org/10.1007/979-8-8688-1273-6

Managing Director, Apress Media LLC: Welmoed Spahr
Acquisitions Editor: Aditee Mirashi
Desk Editor: James Markham
Editorial Project Manager: Kripa Joseph

Cover image designed by eStudioCalamar

Distributed to the book trade worldwide by Springer Science+Business Media New York, 1 New York Plaza, Suite 4600, New York, NY 10004-1562, USA. Phone 1-800-SPRINGER, fax (201) 348-4505, e-mail orders-ny@springer-sbm.com, or visit www.springeronline.com. Apress Media, LLC is a California LLC and the sole member (owner) is Springer Science + Business Media Finance Inc (SSBM Finance Inc). SSBM Finance Inc is a **Delaware** corporation.

For information on translations, please e-mail booktranslations@springernature.com; for reprint, paperback, or audio rights, please e-mail bookpermissions@springernature.com.

Apress titles may be purchased in bulk for academic, corporate, or promotional use. eBook versions and licenses are also available for most titles. For more information, reference our Print and eBook Bulk Sales web page at http://www.apress.com/bulk-sales.

Any source code or other supplementary material referenced by the author in this book is available to readers on GitHub. For more detailed information, please visit https://www.apress.com/gp/services/source-code.

If disposing of this product, please recycle the paper

Table of Contents

About the Author xi

About the Technical Reviewer xiii

Acknowledgment xv

Introduction xvii

Chapter 1: Salesforce Platform Fundamentals 1

Abstract 1

Salesforce: A Brief History 1

An Overview of the Salesforce Platform 3

Types of Objects in Salesforce 5

    Standard Objects 5

    Custom Objects 6

    External Objects 6

    Big Objects 6

    The Differences Between Standard and Custom Objects 6

Getting Started with Lightning Experience 7

    Sales Cloud Editions 8

    Service Cloud Editions 10

    Why Is Understanding Lightning Experience Important? 13

    Sign up for Developer Playground 13

    Navigation Menu 15

    App Launcher 15

    Global Search 17

AppExchange: Apps That Make Life Easier 17

The Benefits of Using AppExchange Apps 19

The Force.com Multitenant Architecture 20

Additional Hands-on Exercises 21

Summary.. 22

Chapter 2: The Underpinnings of Data Modeling 23

Abstract... 23

Metadata: The Core of the Salesforce Platform 23

Look No Further Than Metadata: It's the Key! 24

Why Do We Need Metadata? 25

Understanding the Power of Schema Builder 26

Understanding the Data Model 27

Creating a Custom Field... 28

Managing Field-level Security 30

The Advantages of Using Schema Builder 32

Understanding Relationship Types in Salesforce 33

    Lookup Relationship 33

    Self-Relationship 35

    Master-Detail Relationship 36

    The Differences Between a Master-Detail Relationship and a Lookup Relationship 36

    External Lookup Relationship 37

    Indirect Lookup Relationship 37

    Many-to-Many Relationship 38

    Hierarchal Relationship 39

    Selecting the Appropriate Field Type 39

    Understanding Field Dependencies... 41

    Setting up Field Dependencies.. 43

    Implications of Changing a Field's Type 45

    Exploring External Objects.. 47

Points to Remember 48

Hands-on Exercises 49

Summary.. 51

Chapter 3: Platform Security **53**

Abstract 53

OWD: A Baseline Setting for Objects 53

Understanding the Settings Available for OWD 56

    Predefined OWD for Objects 58

    The Importance of Role Hierarchy 59

    Setting up Role Hierarchies 63

    Record-Sharing Capabilities 74

    Manual Sharing: Share Records on a One-off Basis 75

    Owner-based Sharing: A Way to Share Records Automatically 77

    Apex-Managed Sharing: A Way to Manage Complex Sharing in Seconds 79

    Deferring Sharing Calculations: Postpone Automatic Sharing Recalculation 79

Profiles: A Way to Control Actions Users Can Take on a Record 81

    Types of Profiles 81

Permission Sets 82

    Settings That Can Be Granted Through Permission Sets 83

Points to Remember 87

Hands-on Exercises 89

Summary 92

Chapter 4: Customizing the User Interface **93**

Abstract 93

A Deep Dive into Lightning Experience 93

    The Lightning Experience Navigation Menu 94

    The App Launcher in Lightning Experience 95

    The Home Page 96

    Global Search 97

Creating Dynamic Lightning Pages 99

    Controlling Component Visibility 99

Lightning Page Assignment 102

    Use Case for Custom Buttons and Links 105

Use Case for Custom Actions 108

Points to Remember 109

Hands-on Exercises 110

Summary... 111

Chapter 5: Improving and Enriching Data Quality **113**

Abstract.. 113

Record Types: A Better Way to Handle Varied Business Processes.................... 113

What Are Record Types? 116

How Record Types Control Lightning Record Pages 121

Lookup Filter: Limit the Records That Can Be Shown in a Lookup Window 122

Formula Fields: Small Work, Big Impact 124

Roll-up Summary Field 128

Validation Rules 131

Custom Permissions: A Way to Bypass Validation Rules 134

Points to Remember 138

Hands-on Exercises 139

Summary... 143

Chapter 6: Automating Business Processes **145**

Abstract.. 145

Introduction to Salesforce Flow 145

The Advantages of Using Salesforce Flow... 148

The Salesforce Flow Life Cycle.. 148

An Overview of Salesforce Flow Designer... 149

Different Ways to Launch a Flow 151

Use Case 1: Mortgage Broker Commission Calculator 152

Use Case 2: Delete Unqualified Leads 160

Use Case 3: Update Child Records... 165

Introduction to Approval Processes 169

Wizards to Create an Approval Process... 169

Creating a New Approval Process 170

Final Approval Actions 175

Initial Submission Actions 176

Approval Steps 177

Activating an Approval Process 179

Points to Remember 180

Hands-on Exercises 181

Summary 182

Chapter 7: The Nuts and Bolts of Application Development 183

Abstract 183

The Limits of Declarative Development 183

Business Use Case 1 183

Business Use Case 2 184

Business Use Case 3 186

Use Case Summary 186

Managing the Application Life Cycle 186

Application Governance 187

Application Development 187

Application Operations 187

Sandboxes 187

Developer Sandbox 189

Developer Pro Sandbox 189

Partial Sandbox 189

Full Sandbox 189

Setting up a Sandbox 190

Accessing a Sandbox 192

Deployment 193

Deploy Using Change Sets 193

Deploy Using Packages 201

Points to Remember 201

Hands-on Exercises 202

Summary 204

Chapter 8: The Power of Social Analytics.. **205**

Abstract.. 205

Introduction to Reports 205

    Report Types 206

    Setting up a Custom Report Type 206

    Report Format Types.. 208

Dashboard Components and Its Types 213

    Creating a Dashboard 214

    Making a Dashboard Dynamic... 216

Points to Remember 218

Hands-on Exercises 218

Summary.. 220

Appendix: Answers to Hands-on Exercises **221**

Index... **227**

About the Author

Rakesh Gupta is a seasoned Salesforce Solution Architect known for his strategic expertise in developing and delivering Salesforce solutions across various industries, including public sector, manufacturing, and financial services. With over 14 years of experience in Salesforce development, consulting, and architecture, he has led successful implementations of complex, large-scale solutions. He is a nine-time Salesforce MVP and a member of the MVP Hall of Fame, recognized for his exceptional contributions to the Salesforce community.

Rakesh is also a well-known author, speaker, and coach, having written multiple books and over 300 articles on Salesforce Flow, CRM Analytics, Lightning Web Component, Apex, and automation best practices. As co-host of the popular Automation Hour webinar series, he shares practical insights and advanced techniques to help Salesforce users minimize code usage and maximize platform efficiency. He is passionate about empowering individuals and organizations to achieve their goals through Salesforce and has personally trained over 3,100 professionals globally.

Actively engaged in the Salesforce ecosystem, Rakesh co-leads the Mumbai Architect User Group in India and maintains the Automation Champion blog, a go-to resource for Salesforce automation. When not working, he enjoys cooking, movies, and spending time with family and friends in Dallas, Texas. Follow him on X (@rakeshistom) for insights into his latest projects, blog posts, and Salesforce tips and tricks.

About the Technical Reviewer

Venkata Karthik Penikalapati is a seasoned software developer with over a decade of expertise in designing and managing intricate distributed systems, data pipelines, and artificial intelligence/machine learning applications. Armed with a master's degree in computer science from the University at Buffalo, his knowledge spans the realms of machine learning, data engineering, and workflow orchestration. Venkata thrives in the world of distributed systems, continually pushing the boundaries of innovation.

Currently, Karthik is a valuable member of the Salesforce team within the Search Cloud division. Here, he's at the forefront of cutting-edge developments, spearheading the integration of the latest advancements in artificial intelligence.

Acknowledgment

First and foremost, I extend my heartfelt gratitude to my parents, Kedar Nath Gupta and Madhuri Gupta; my wife, Meenakshi; my sister, Sarika Gupta; and my brother-in-law, Manish Kumar, for their patience and unwavering support as I took on yet another challenge that reduced the time I could spend with them. They have been my inspiration, motivation, and driving force behind my quest to expand my knowledge and advance my career.

I sincerely thank Apress for giving me the incredible opportunity to share my knowledge through this book.

A special thanks goes out to all my well-wishers and friends. I extend a particularly heartfelt thanks to the reviewer—your insights and feedback have been instrumental in bringing this book to life. Finally, I am deeply thankful to every member of the Salesforce Ohana for being a constant source of inspiration and learning.

Introduction

Salesforce is one of the most sought-after and rapidly growing enterprise software platforms today. *Salesforce Platform App Builder Certification Companion: Mastering the Essentials for Exam Success and Beyond* is a hands-on resource designed to support both beginners with a foundational understanding of Salesforce and seasoned professionals aiming to elevate their expertise and achieve Salesforce-certified Platform App Builder status. This book is packed with real-world examples to deepen your comprehension of the Salesforce ecosystem.

Not only will this guide help you pass the Salesforce Platform App Builder certification exam, but it will also introduce you to advanced concepts, including platform security, customizing the Lightning interface, automation, social features, the application development life cycle, and more.

To get started, all you need is a curious mind, a computer with a modern web browser, and a free Salesforce developer org. You can sign up for one at developer. salesforce.com/signup. Prepare for an exciting journey—let's dive in!

The book is structured into eight chapters.

- Chapter 1 lays the groundwork with the fundamentals of the Salesforce platform.

- Chapter 2 delves into Salesforce data modeling.

- Chapter 3 explores platform security in detail.

- Chapter 4 takes you on a tour of the Lightning Experience.

- Chapter 5 focuses on business process automation.

- Chapter 6 provides an in-depth exploration of Salesforce Flow.

- Chapter 7 covers the application development lifecycle.

- Chapter 8 highlights Salesforce's analytics capabilities.

Each chapter concludes with hands-on exercises designed to reinforce what you've learned. Answers to these exercises can be found in the appendix.

Drawing on my years of experience with Salesforce, I have carefully identified the key areas that will be most beneficial for you. Whether you're just starting your Salesforce journey or looking to broaden your skills, I hope this book serves as a valuable resource. Enjoy the experience.

CHAPTER 1

Salesforce Platform Fundamentals

Abstract

This book takes a hands-on approach to explain concepts you need to know to prepare for the Salesforce-certified platform app builder credential. New and intermediate developers need to have experience designing, building, and implementing custom applications using the declarative customization capabilities of the Salesforce platform, so let's get the ball rolling.

This chapter starts with an overview of the Salesforce platform and Sales and Service Cloud product offerings. It then takes a close look at Lightning Experience and navigation items. The second half of this chapter examines how AppExchange is changing the way customers use Salesforce and studies the basics of the Salesforce platform.

Salesforce: A Brief History

In 1999, a few former Oracle executives (including Mark Benioff and Parker Harris) started Salesforce with a vision to provide cloud-based CRM systems to customers. CRM stands for *customer relationship management*. It allows companies to manage relationships with their customers and prospects, and it enables them to track all interactions, touchpoints, and so on. You can easily connect CRM with social media, phone, email, and third-party channels to collect information about customers and prospects.

1

R. Gupta, *Salesforce Platform App Builder Certification Companion*, Certification Study Companion Series

As it happens, a business may start with one vision in mind and, later, as it succeeds, it may add other products or services. For example, Apple Inc. started with one offering—computers—and later it added Macintosh, iPhone, iPad, and so on to its offerings. The same business principle applied to Salesforce. As customers started to use its CRM system, the company expanded its offerings from Sales Cloud to include Service Cloud, Marketing Cloud, Integration Cloud, and more. In the past decade, Salesforce acquired more than 45 companies and expanded its cloud offerings. Now, Salesforce. com, Inc. has Sales, Service, Community, Marketing, Commerce, and Integration Clouds, as well as many other products. As a result, Salesforce is no longer *just* a CRM platform.

To give you an overview of how Salesforce has improved the user experience over time, Figure 1-1 shows what the Salesforce user interface looked like when I started my journey in 2011.

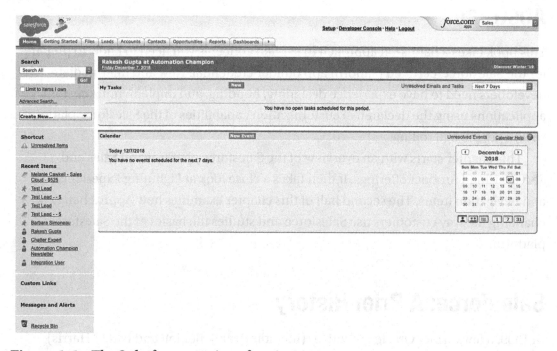

Figure 1-1. *The Salesforce user interface in 2011*

Figure 1-2 depicts what the user interface looks like now. What a difference eight years makes! Now, Salesforce offers many ways to customize screens dynamically based on logged-in users. I talk about this more in Chapter 4.

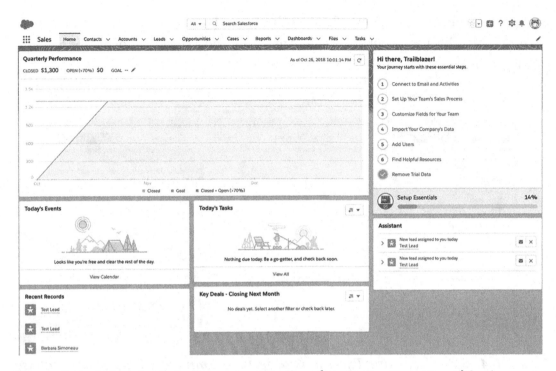

Figure 1-2. *What the Salesforce user interface (Lightning Experience) looks like today*

An Overview of the Salesforce Platform

Let's take a close look at how Salesforce stores data. Fundamentally, Salesforce uses spreadsheet concepts to organize data behind the scenes. It is similar to a database table. Salesforce fields are similar to database columns, and Salesforce records are similar to database rows (see Figure 1-3).

First	Last Name	Company	Email
Rakesh	Gupta	Automation Champion	info@achamp.co
Susan	McDermott	Gurukul On Cloud	susan@gurukuloncloud.com

Figure 1-3. *The similarity between how Excel and Salesforce store data*

Salesforce organizes customer data into objects and records. For example, think of a tab on a spreadsheet as an *object*, a column as a *field*, and a single row of data as a *record* (see Figure 1-4).

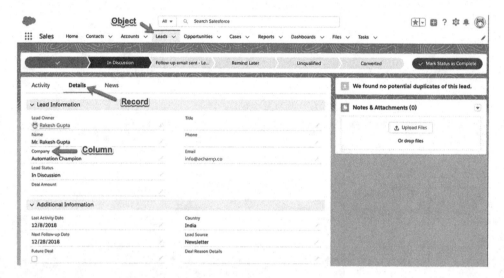

Figure 1-4. *Salesforce stores Excel spreadsheets, columns, and rows in its database*

Now, pause for a minute and think. Do you understand what an object, a field, and a record are? If yes, then answer the following exercise question.

HANDS-ON EXERCISE 1

Miranda Moonilal is working as a receptionist at GurukulonCloud (GoC). At GoC, they use a spreadsheet to store the details of a person's visit to its office. Miranda has a spreadsheet that contains 21 rows, including column names. If you upload the file to Salesforce, how many records will Salesforce create?

a. 21

b. 20

c. 22

d. None

If your answer is correct, it means you have a solid, basic understanding of how Salesforce transposes spreadsheets to objects and records. To see the correct answer, go to the answer appendix at the end of this book.

Types of Objects in Salesforce

Objects are a key component in the Salesforce architecture. They provide the structure to store data and then display the data via the user interface to allow users to interact with the data. Salesforce provides the following types of objects.

- Standard objects

- Custom objects

- External objects

- Big objects

Standard Objects

After you set up a Salesforce org, you'll see that it comes with *standard objects*, which are provided as a core CRM structure. The objects include Lead, Account, Contact, Opportunity, Campaign, and more. They are the database tables that contain the records in any standard tab, such as Leads, Accounts, Contacts, Opportunities, Campaigns, and so on.

- **Lead**: A Lead object contains a prospect (not yet qualified) interested in your products or offerings.

- **Account**: An Account object stores data regarding the customers (and their company) with whom you're doing business.

- **Contact**: The Contact object includes people who work for your customers' company.

- **Opportunity**: The Opportunity object contains qualified leads. These leads are people who have talked to your sales team, expressed interest in continuing the conversation, and maybe even agreed to hear a sales pitch or look over a proposal. Opportunities are always associated with an account.

Custom Objects

In addition to standard objects, Salesforce allows you to create *custom objects* to store data specific to your organization. Because the data is specific to your organization, you may not be able to store org-specific data within the confines of a standard object. Custom objects are ideal for representing entities that are not represented appropriately by any standard object. An example is a custom object that stores employee timesheets, which doesn't come out of the box. Custom objects are usually identified by a __c suffix.

External Objects

External objects are similar to custom objects. They allow you to map the data stored outside of your Salesforce organization using Salesforce Connect. For example, you may have data stored in an enterprise resource planning (ERP) system. You can access this data in Salesforce in real time through external objects using Salesforce Connect. External objects are usually identified by a __x suffix.

Big Objects

Big objects in Salesforce function similarly to custom objects, enabling the storage and management of vast amounts of data, often running into billions of rows. They are particularly useful for archiving Salesforce data or integrating data from external systems. Despite their size, big objects allow real-time data access within Salesforce. These objects are typically denoted by a __b suffix.

The Differences Between Standard and Custom Objects

Table 1-1 highlights the differences between standard and custom objects.

Table 1-1. *Standard Object vs. Custom Object*

Standard Object	Custom Object
Can't delete	Can delete
Can't change the Grant Access Using Hierarchies sharing access	Can change the Grant Access Using Hierarchies sharing access
Can't truncate standard objects	Can truncate custom objects
Typically have predefined names (e.g., Account, Contact)	User-defined names start with a __c suffix
Automatically available in Salesforce orgs	Created via the Salesforce Setup UI, Custom Object from Spreadsheet, or Metadata API

HANDS-ON EXERCISE 2

Pamela Kline is working as a system administrator at GoC. She needs some help identifying the custom object in the following options. Which answer will you give to Pamela?

    a.   CampaignMember

    b.   Leave_Balance__c

    c.   Order__x

    d.   Lead

To see the correct answer, go to the answer appendix at the end of this book.

Getting Started with Lightning Experience

Lightning Experience is a productive user interface designed to help sales teams close deals faster and sell smarter. Lightning Experience is used to create a consistent user interface on all devices—from desktop to mobile. Lightning Experience, in a nutshell, is faster, better, and smarter.

A few years back, Salesforce announced Lightning Editions for Sales and Service Clouds. Lightning Editions is a completely reimagined packaging of Sales and Service Clouds. For a relatively small increase in price, Lightning Editions offers a host of additional functionality to customers, thereby increasing their productivity several-fold. Let's take a look at the Sales Cloud and Service Cloud editions.

Sales Cloud Editions

Sales Cloud is a product designed to automate an organization's sales process. By implementing Sales Cloud, an organization can boost its sales rep productivity. Sales Cloud includes core CRM objects such as Campaign, Lead, Account, Contact, Opportunity, Order, Report, Dashboard, and so on. Salesforce offers various Sales Cloud editions to suit the business needs of varied organizations (see Figure 1-5).

Compare Sales Cloud editions and features.

Top features		Starter Suite $25 user/month	Pro Suite $100 user/month	Enterprise $165 user/month	Unlimited $330 user/month	Einstein 1 Sales $500 user/month
Account, Contact, Lead, and Opportunity Management	ⓘ	✓	✓	✓	✓	✓
Advanced Forecast & Pipeline Management	ⓘ	—	—	✓	✓	✓
Sales Engagement & Conversation Intelligence*	ⓘ	—	—	Available for purchase	✓	✓
Premier Success Plan	ⓘ	—	Available for purchase	Available for purchase	✓	✓
Generative AI	ⓘ			Available for purchase	Available for purchase	✓
Unified Data	ⓘ	—	—	Available for purchase	Available for purchase	✓
Sales Planning, Programs & Collaboration	ⓘ	—	—	Available for purchase	Available for purchase	✓

Figure 1-5. *Comparison of Sales Cloud editions*

- **Starter Suite**: The Salesforce Starter Suite is a comprehensive package designed to provide small to medium-sized businesses with the essential tools they need to manage customer relationships, streamline operations, and drive growth. For each Starter Suite edition license, organizations currently pay US$25 per user per month.

- **Pro Suite**: The Pro Suite edition is designed for small- and medium-sized businesses. It provides CRM functionality, including marketing, sales, and service automation. You can create a limited number of processes, role hierarchies, profiles, permission sets, and record types. For each Pro Suite edition license, organizations currently pay US$100 per user per month.

- **Enterprise**: The Enterprise edition is designed for companies with complex business requirements. It includes all the features available in the Professional edition, plus it provides advanced customization capabilities through Apex programming and web service application programming interfaces (APIs) to integrate with third-party systems. For each Enterprise edition license, organizations pay US$165 per user per month.

- **Unlimited**: The Unlimited edition includes all Salesforce.com features for an entire company. It provides all the features of the Enterprise edition along with a new level of platform flexibility for managing and sharing all information on demand. The key features of the Lightning Unlimited edition are premier support, full mobile access, increased storage limits, and more. In addition, it also includes Work.com, Service Cloud, Knowledge Base, a live-chat feature, multiple sandboxes, and unlimited custom app development. For each Unlimited edition license, organizations pay US$330 per user per month.

- **Einstein 1 Sales**: Salesforce Einstein 1 Sales is a comprehensive AI-driven sales solution designed to enhance the capabilities of the Sales Cloud by providing predictive insights, automation, and advanced analytics. This suite leverages the power of Salesforce's Einstein AI to help sales teams work smarter, close deals faster, and improve overall sales performance. For each Einstein 1 Sales edition license, organizations pay US$500 per user per month.

Note   When purchasing Salesforce.com licenses, organizations must negotiate with a Salesforce account executive to get the maximum number of sandboxes. To learn more about these license types, please visit the Salesforce website at www.salesforce.com/sales/pricing/.

HANDS-ON EXERCISE 3

GoC has recently signed an agreement with a customer, Universal Containers (UC), to implement Salesforce Sales Cloud for them. UC wants to integrate Sales Cloud with their ERP system. At the minimum, which Sales Cloud edition should UC purchase?

    a.   Unlimited

    b.   Professional

    c.   Enterprise

    d.   Pro Suite

To see the correct answer, go to the answer appendix at the end of this book.

Service Cloud Editions

Service Cloud is a product designed to streamline an organization's support process. By implementing this product, an organization can streamline support channels and consolidate all communication in Salesforce, so support agents can channel their expertise into solving customer issues rather than hunting for information (see Figure 1-6). Salesforce provides various ways customers can connect with support agents, including live chat, computer telephony integration (CTI), video chat, social media, Salesforce Community, and so on.

Compare editions and top features.

Top features.

		Starter Suite $25 user/month	Pro Suite $100 user/month	Enterprise $165 user/month	Unlimited $330 user/month	Einstein 1 Service $500 user/month
Case Management	ⓘ	✓	✓	✓	✓	✓
Omni-Channel Routing	ⓘ	—	✓	✓	✓	✓
Knowledge Management	ⓘ	✓	✓	—	✓	✓
Service Contracts and Entitlements	ⓘ	—	✓	✓	✓	✓
Premier Success Plan*	ⓘ	—	Available for Purchase	Available for Purchase	✓	✓
Einstein for Service	ⓘ	—	—	Available for Purchase	Available for Purchase	✓
Unified Voice & Messaging	ⓘ	—	—	—	—	✓

Show more features ▼

Figure 1-6. *Comparison of Service Cloud Lightning editions*

- **Pro Suite**: The Pro Suite edition is designed for small- and medium-sized businesses. It provides CRM functionality, including marketing, sales, and service automation. You can create a limited number of processes, role hierarchies, profiles, permission sets, and record types. For each Pro Suite edition license, organizations currently pay US$100 per user per month.

- **Pro Suite**: The Pro Suite edition is designed for small- and medium-sized businesses. It includes features such as case management, CTI integration, mobile access, solution management, content library, reports, and analytics, along with sales features such as opportunity management and forecasting. You can create a limited number of processes, role hierarchies, profiles, permission sets, and record types. For each Professional edition license, organizations currently pay US$100 per user per month.

- **Enterprise:** The Enterprise edition is designed for companies with complex business requirements. It includes all the features available in the Professional edition, plus it provides advanced customization capabilities through Apex programming and web service APIs to integrate with other systems. It also includes Service Console, Service Contract, Knowledge Base, and Entitlement Management. For each Enterprise edition license, organizations currently pay US$165 per user per month.

- **Unlimited:** The Unlimited edition includes all Salesforce features for an entire enterprise. It provides all the features of the Enterprise edition and a new level of platform flexibility for managing and sharing all information on demand. The key features of the Lightning Unlimited edition include premier support, full mobile access, unlimited custom apps, increased storage limits, and more. It also includes Work.com, Service Cloud, Knowledge Base, live chat, multiple sandboxes, and unlimited custom app development.

- **Einstein 1 Sales:** Salesforce Einstein 1 Sales is a comprehensive AI-driven sales solution designed to enhance the capabilities of the Sales Cloud by providing predictive insights, automation, and advanced analytics. This suite leverages the power of Salesforce's Einstein AI to help sales teams work smarter, close deals faster, and improve overall sales performance. For each Einstein 1 Sales edition license, organizations pay US$500 per user per month.

Note   When purchasing licenses, organizations must negotiate with a Salesforce account executive to get the maximum number of sandboxes. To learn more about these license types, visit the Salesforce website at `www.salesforce.com/service/pricing/`.

Why Is Understanding Lightning Experience Important?

Lightning Experience is a new user interface that includes the artificial intelligence (AI) feature called Salesforce Einstein AI. It is easier to customize, faster to use, and smart enough to help you to close deals. Using Lightning Experience, you can enhance sales and support rep experience and productivity. You can create highly dynamic pages easily without writing a single line of code, which is quite cumbersome in Salesforce Classic, to say the least.

Sign up for Developer Playground

Salesforce offers free developer playground accounts to all administrators and developers. You can use the Salesforce playground to learn Salesforce by practicing new concepts and building custom applications. Do not use Salesforce production/live instances to practice concepts. You can always use a Salesforce sandbox or free developer account (see Figure 1-7) to practice the examples covered in this book. If you do not own a developer account, create a new one by visiting `https://developer.salesforce.com/signup/`.

Figure 1-7. *Sign-up form for the Salesforce platform development environment*

After you register for a developer account, Salesforce.com, Inc. sends login details to the email address you provided during registration. Follow the instructions in your email to get started with Salesforce. After a successful login, you are redirected to the Home tab (in the Lightning Experience user interface).

Navigation Menu

Using the navigation menu, you can jump from one tab to another tab (see Figure 1-8). These tabs are generally associated with the object's or app's tabs. Salesforce also allows you to customize the navigation menu to include both standard, custom, and external objects.

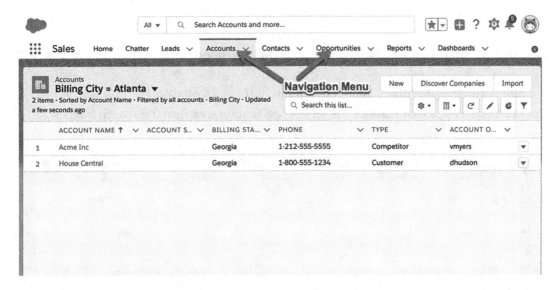

Figure 1-8. An example of a navigation menu

App Launcher

Using App Launcher, you can switch between applications (see Figure 1-9). For example, in your Salesforce org, you may have several standard and custom applications. Let's suppose you are in the Sales app, and you want to switch to the Marketing app. You do this using App Launcher.

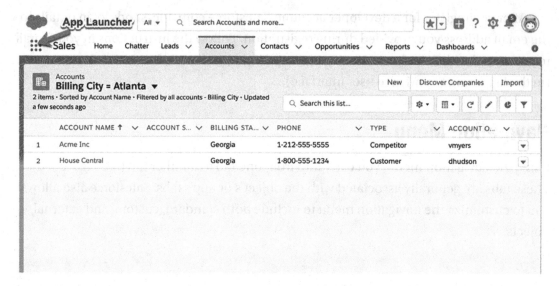

Figure 1-9. *An example of how to access App Launcher*

App Launcher provides a search feature to find apps by name. For example, if you want to find all apps that contain the letters "es", just type **es** into the search box, as shown in Figure 1-10.

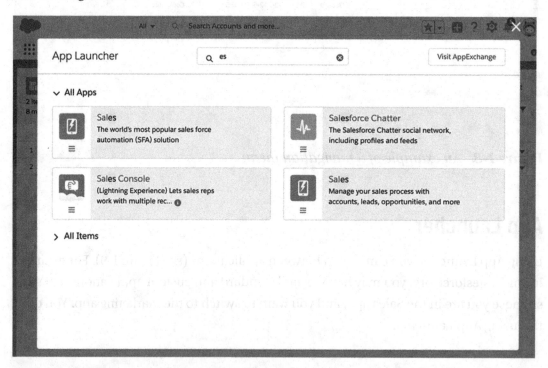

Figure 1-10. *App Launcher's search feature*

Global Search

Using the global search capability, you can find a record easily by breaking your search terms. The global search box is available at the top of every page. When you click it, you'll see a drop-down of all your recent items (see Figure 1-11).

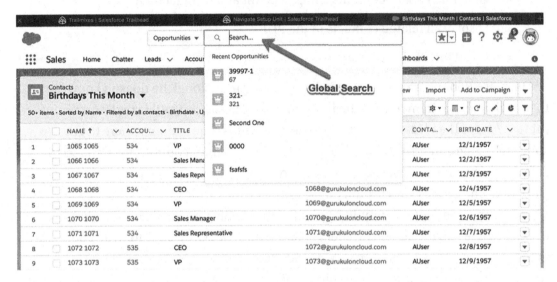

Figure 1-11. *An example of how to access the global search feature*

It is also possible to limit the search boundaries to a specific object. For example, the screenshot in Figure 1-11 is limited to the `Opportunities` object.

AppExchange: Apps That Make Life Easier

Most of us use several apps a day on our phones. These apps make our lives easier. For example, I use the Nest thermostat app to control the temperature of my home from my phone, even though I am not at home. It helps me save on my energy bill.

You can download such apps from the Google Play Store or App Store and install them on your phone. The same principles apply to Salesforce. When a customer has a particular business requirement, they have three options: they can download an app from AppExchange, develop it from scratch, or pay a third party to build it.

Let's look at the following business scenario: Robin Guzman just bought the Salesforce Lightning Enterprise edition. He has been working as a Salesforce administrator for a few months when he receives the following requirements from his manager.

- Generate PDF documents using Account and Contact data

- Display all related contacts in the PDF

- Email the PDF to customers

Because Robin is an inexperienced Salesforce professional, he doesn't know how to provide the requirements. So, he hops onto the Salesforce Trailblazer Community (https://trailhead.salesforce.com/) and posts his requirements there to get some help. Salesforce Trailblazer Community is a customer community managed by Salesforce.com, Inc. that allows customers to interact with other customers, partners, Salesforce enthusiasts, and product managers.

Someone from the community suggested that Robin write code to provide the capabilities required. The problem is Robin does not know how to write code in Salesforce. Another person suggested that Robin use Conga Composer—an AppExchange app—to meet his requirements.

Robin is very excited about this advice, and he navigates to the Salesforce AppExchange website (https://appexchange.salesforce.com). At first, he was overwhelmed to see thousands of applications uploaded by partners, interdependent software vendors (ISVs), and consultants. He also learns that some apps are free, whereas others must be purchased. Because Robin is looking for Conga, he types **Conga** in the search box and finds the application, as shown in Figure 1-12.

Conga Composer allows Robin to generate documents automatically by using Salesforce data that he can then send to his customers.

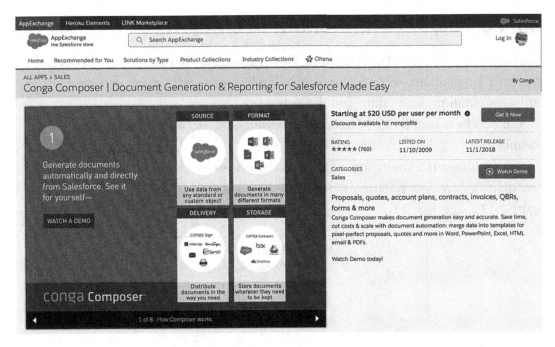

Figure 1-12. *An overview of the Conga Composer app in AppExchange*

The Benefits of Using AppExchange Apps

There are certain benefits to using AppExchange over custom development.

- **Development cost savings**: AppExchange apps save thousands of dollars that a company would have to spend to build a custom app.

- **Quick deployment**: There is no need to wait for weeks until developers deploy a custom application. It is very easy to configure AppExchange apps. You can start using an app from AppExchange within a few hours of downloading it in your instance.

- **Secure**: AppExchange apps are not only fast to install, but all code is also tested and passed by Salesforce, so customers can be assured that all apps go through a rigorous security review process.

- **Upgradable**: Usually, paid apps are automatically upgraded when vendors release an enhancement.

- **Well documented**: AppExchange apps are well documented, which may not be the case if you develop a custom app.

The Force.com Multitenant Architecture

Salesforce is built on top of the Lightning Platform, a cloud-based platform to develop enterprise applications. As a developer, you don't have to worry about network, hardware, platform maintenance, or downtime.

You may have heard that Salesforce is a *multitenant architecture*. But what does that mean?

In a multitenant architecture, a single system serves as a base service to all customers. This means system resources are shared among all customers (see Figure 1-13).

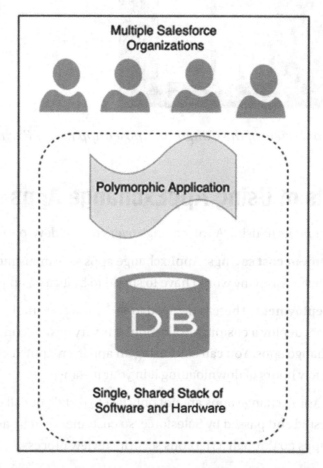

Figure 1-13. *Multitenant architectures control how resources are shared among customers*

Let's take a real-world example. If you live in a multistory building, you have your own space (say, a two-bedroom apartment). Other people live in the same building, too. As a result, there is a common space everyone must share.

The same concept applies to Salesforce. Salesforce provides all organizations with a single copy of an app that runs on the same Salesforce server. Customers are allowed to customize an org according to their business needs. Because several customers share the same Salesforce server, Salesforce applies some limits to make sure no one uses more resources than their allotted share. In formal terms, this is called a *governance limit*. Governance limits make sure an organization does not hit a threshold that might negatively affect the performance of the system as a whole, thereby affecting not only the organization that hit the threshold but also all other "tenants" as well.

Additional Hands-on Exercises

The following exercises give you more practice using the Lightning Platform. Because these are straightforward exercises, no "answers" are included in the appendix.

1. Explore Lightning Experience and find the Setup section.

2. Create one Lead, one Account, and one Contact record.

3. Switch to the Service app using AppLauncher.

4. Find all records with the name *Acme*.

5. Update your profile image in Salesforce.

6. Log out of Salesforce.

7. Explore the Conga Composer app and find the reviews posted by other customers.

8. Install the Conga Composer app in your free developer account for admin only.

9. Navigate to the Conga Composer app in Salesforce.

Summary

This chapter studied the Salesforce platform, including how Salesforce stores data in objects and fields. It also examined various Salesforce editions available on the market for sales and service clouds. Furthermore, it looked at a high-level overview of Lightning Experience. Finally, it examined the advantages of AppExchange over custom development, and you learned about Force.com architectures.

CHAPTER 2

The Underpinnings of Data Modeling

Abstract

The previous chapter looked at the Salesforce platform, including the Salesforce editions for Sales and Service Clouds. It took a high-level look at Lightning Experience, discussed the advantages of AppExchange over custom development, and studied the Force.com architecture.

This chapter reviews metadata and Schema Builder, examines the different types of relationships in Salesforce, and explores a few real-world examples. The chapter also discusses various field types and studies a use case of external objects.

Metadata: The Core of the Salesforce Platform

How is Salesforce able to deliver the best customer experience? What enables the Salesforce platform to be highly customizable? How is Salesforce able to separate customer data, customer customization (for example, list views, reports, and fields), and platform architecture? As you saw in Chapter 1, a multitenant architecture is a software architecture module in which multiple instances of software run on a single physical server. The server then serves multiple tenants. Apart from the Salesforce multitenant architecture, what else holds the key?

R. Gupta, *Salesforce Platform App Builder Certification Companion, Certification Study Companion Series*

Look No Further Than Metadata: It's the Key!

Metadata? What is that? I was stumped. I started researching and was awed by it! I spent hours peeling away the layers to achieve mastery over the concept, for it is, indeed, the key to understanding how Salesforce is able to deliver the best customer experience!

In a nutshell, metadata is information about data! Wait a minute! What? Yes, it is that simple. And yet, it is a complicated concept. So, let me take a crack at explaining it by providing three examples involving Pamela Kline, a Salesforce administrator at GoC.

- On December 17, Pamela traveled from San Francisco to the Dallas–Fort Worth (DFW) Airport. At the airport, she met Julie Ball. Julie works at UC as vice president (VP) of sales. Julie likes to travel and explore new cities.

- On December 24, Pamela met Jessica Murphy at Costco. Jessica is working at Northern Trail Outfitters as a store manager. Jessica likes to learn about new technology.

- On December 26, Pamela met Jana Mickel, chief executive officer (CEO) of Acme Nonprofit, at Starbucks. Jana likes to inspire people by doing charity work on weekends.

Comb through the three previous scenarios carefully! When you do, one thing should stand out: the structural information in all three examples is the same, but the descriptive information is different. Table 2-1 highlights the concept.

Table 2-1. *How to Store Metadata in a Table Format*

Name	Place They Meet	Date They Meet	Company	Position	Interest
Julie Ball	DFW Airport	December 17	Universal Containers	VP of Sales	Travel
Jessica Murphy	Costco	December 24	Northern Trail Outfitters	Store manager	New technology
Jana Mickel	Starbucks	December 26	Acme Nonprofit	CEO	Charity work

Table 2-1 is just a table *until you realize it consists of metadata and data*. Metadata is column labels—in this case, Name, Place They Meet, Date They Meet, Company, Position, and Interest. The data, however, includes Julie Ball, DFW Airport, December 17, UC, VP of Sales, travel, and so on. In other words, data is information *within* a column that is *different in each row*.

Let's look at another example to acquire an understanding of the difference between metadata and data.

- Metadata about music CDs includes genre, composer, location of recording, record label, and so on.

- Metadata about books includes subject, author, publisher, language, and year of publication.

- Metadata about photographs includes the photographer's name, the date a photo was taken, the subject, and the location.

Why Do We Need Metadata?

Metadata helps us find things. It is used to organize data! Let's look at an example to understand how metadata helps in real-life situations.

In a bookstore, you can find books by author (see Figure 2-1).

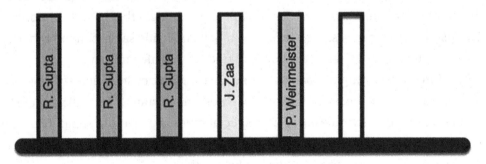

Figure 2-1. *How to organize books in a bookstore*

In a music store, you can find music CDs by artist name (see Figure 2-2).

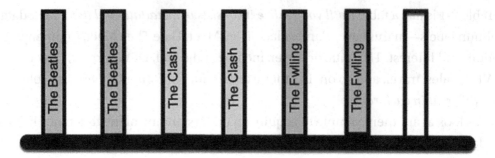

Figure 2-2. *How to organize CDs in a music store*

When renting a film, you can find movies by genre (see Figure 2-3).

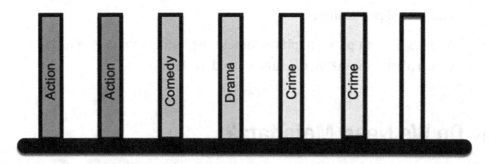

Figure 2-3. *How to organize movies by genre*

In addition to organizing data, metadata also helps to secure your organization's data. In an organization, users need permission to access data that belongs to someone else. For instance, when accessing a lead, Sarah Bell, an inside sales team member, must request access to a record so she can view and update the information.

In Salesforce, everything you access—from custom tabs, custom fields, reports, and so on—is metadata. It is the backbone of your Salesforce instance, with all your custom and standard functionality. Salesforce uses special metadata layers to separate customer customizations so that, despite upgrading the platform three times a year, it does not modify customer data or customizations inadvertently.

Understanding the Power of Schema Builder

Schema Builder is a tool that can be used to visualize and edit a data model. The tool comes in handy when you want to understand and design data models that are highly customized and complex.

Schema Builder is an interactive drag-and-drop tool that can be used to perform the following actions.

- View relationships between objects

- View the following objects on the canvas

  - Standard objects

  - Custom objects

  - System objects, including User, Task, Event, and Activity

- Create and delete custom objects

- Modify properties of custom objects

- Create and delete custom fields

- Modify properties of custom fields

- Manage fields permission

Understanding the Data Model

As mentioned, Schema Builder can be used to understand the relationship between objects, or you can simply explore only one object by adding it to the canvas. Let's look at Schema Builder via a business use case.

Robin Guzman just bought the Salesforce Lightning Enterprise edition. He has been working as a Salesforce administrator for a few months. Recently, he got an assignment to implement campaign management, and he wants to understand the relationships between the objects used in campaign management (Lead, Contact, Campaign, and Campaign Members).

Robin performs the following steps to meet the task's requirements.

1. He clicks Setup (gear icon) ➤ Setup Home ➤ Data ➤ Objects and Fields ➤ Schema Builder and then navigates to the Objects tab.

2. He then selects the objects—Lead, Contact, Campaign, and Campaign Member—to display on the canvas (see Figure 2-4).

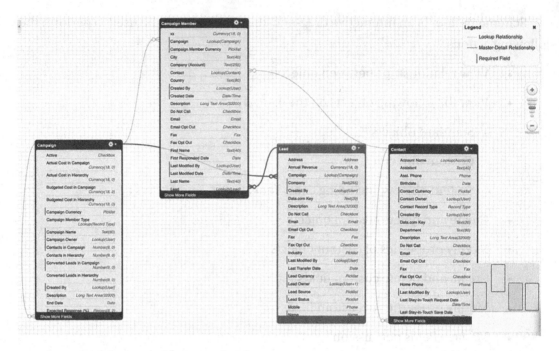

Figure 2-4. *Selecting objects to display*

By looking at the screenshot shown in Figure 2-4, Robin understands *how these objects are connected*. He realizes that `Campaign Member` is the *junction object* that *connects* `Lead` and `Contact` to the `Campaign` object.

Creating a Custom Field

Custom fields are unique to your business needs. Creating custom fields allows you to store information that is unique to your organization. These fields can be added, amended, and deleted. Custom fields are usually identified by a __c suffix.

Let's return to our business scenario. Robin now understands how objects within a campaign connect to each other. He is thrilled by the power of Schema Builder. Having mastered the concepts behind it, Robin is ready to tackle the following new requirements.

- Add a custom field to the `Lead` object to store a credit score.

- Set the field length to 1 and the decimal places to 0.

Robin uses Schema Builder to fulfill these requirements as follows.

1. He clicks Setup (gear icon) ➤ Setup Home ➤ Data ➤ Objects and Fields ➤ Schema Builder and then navigates to the Objects tab.

2. He selects "Lead to display on the canvas".

3. Then, he clicks the Elements tab.

4. Next, Robin selects the Number field and drags and drops it onto an object on the canvas. This action opens a window, where he enters the following details.

    a. **Field Label**: This is the label for the custom field; in this case, he enters **Credit Score** as the label.

    b. **Field Name**: This is the name of the field, which autopopulates based on the label.

    c. **Description**: This is meaningful text so another developer or administrator can easily understand why this custom field was created.

    d. **Help Text**: This is meaningful help text; whenever users hover over this field, they can easily understand what they must enter in this field

    e. **Default Value**: A value for this custom field is inserted automatically when a new record is created.

    f. **Length**: This is field length; in this case, Robin enters **1.**

    g. **Decimal Places**: This is the number of digits to display after the decimal point; in this case, he enters **0.**

    h. **Required**: This is an option for making a field required. In this case, Robin knows the best practice is to use a validation rule to make a field required; therefore, he does not select this check box.

    i. **Unique**: This is an option for making a field unique. In our case, Robin does not need it to be a unique field, so he does not select the check box.

    j. **External ID**: This is an option for making this field a unique record identifier from an external system.

The result of these actions is shown in Figure 2-5.

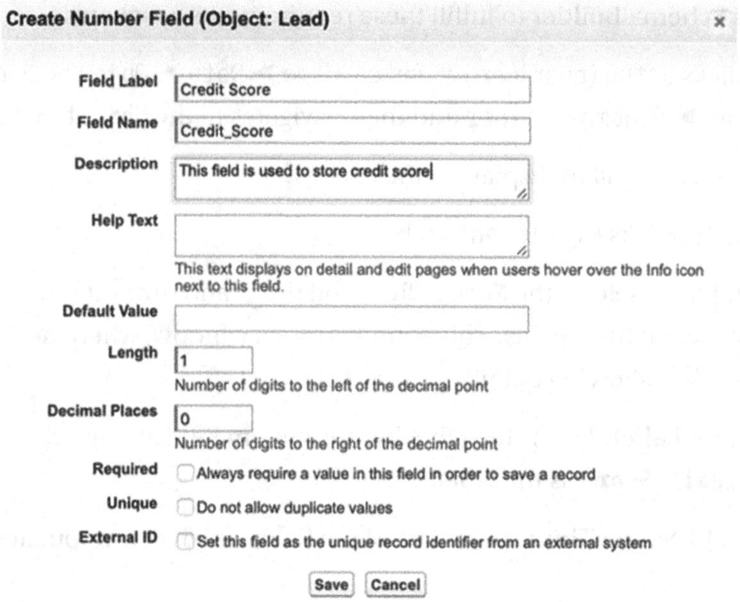

Create Number Field (Object: Lead)   ×

Field Label	Credit Score
Field Name	Credit_Score
Description	This field is used to store credit score
Help Text	

This text displays on detail and edit pages when users hover over the Info icon next to this field.

Default Value	
Length	1

Number of digits to the left of the decimal point

Decimal Places	0

Number of digits to the right of the decimal point

Required   ☐ Always require a value in this field in order to save a record

Unique   ☐ Do not allow duplicate values

External ID   ☐ Set this field as the unique record identifier from an external system

Save   Cancel

Figure 2-5. *Screen to create a custom field using Schema Builder*

5. Finally, Robin clicks the Save button.

Tip   Instead of creating new custom fields, standard fields can be used by renaming the label.

Managing Field-level Security

It is a myth that Schema Builder can't be used to set field-level security. Let's set field-level security using Schema Builder and put the myth to rest once and for all using our business scenario.

Robin is pleased. He added his first field using Schema Builder. Now, he must tackle another requirement: grant the Credit Score field Read/Write access to the following profiles.

- System administrator

- API user (custom profile)

To fulfill this task, Robin performs the following steps using Schema Builder.

1. He right-clicks the Credit Score custom field.

2. He selects Manage Field Permissions, as shown in Figure 2-6.

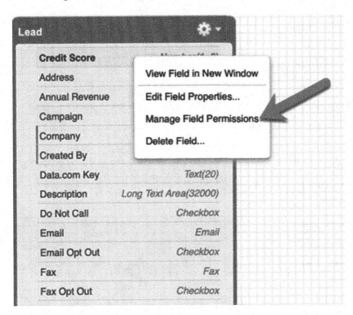

Figure 2-6. *Screen to manage field permission using Schema Builder*

3. These actions open a window that Robin uses to set up field-level security based on the stipulated requirements. He grants access to the System Administrator and API User only (see Figure 2-7), and then clicks the Save button.

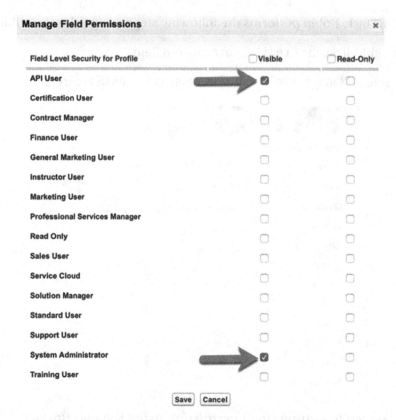

Figure 2-7. *Screen to grant field permission using Schema Builder*

The Advantages of Using Schema Builder

Schema Builder has the following advantages over traditional approaches to create, edit, and delete objects and fields.

- It eliminates the need to click from page to page to create custom objects and fields.

- It is a graphical way to analyze relationships between objects.

- It adds fields and objects without leaving Schema Builder.

- It saves time when creating multiple fields.

Understanding Relationship Types in Salesforce

When you create a relationship between two objects, you select a relationship type to determine how closely associated you want the related records to be. You can connect a standard object to another standard or custom object and vice versa. For example, if you have a custom object named Event (where you store information about upcoming events) and you want to associate it with another custom object, Registrant (to store information about registrants for a particular event), you can associate the registrant records with the respective event record.

These relationship types also control how *record sharing*, *data deletion*, and *required fields* in the page layout are handled. The following are the types of relationships that can be established between objects.

- Lookup relationship

- Self-relationship

- Master detail relationship

- External lookup relationship

- Indirect lookup relationship

- Many-to-many relationship (junction object)

- Hierarchical relationship

Lookup Relationship

Lookup is a loosely connected relationship among Salesforce objects. This means that if someone deletes the parent record, the child's records remain in the system. In a lookup relationship, both parent and child have separate shared settings (see Figure 2-8).

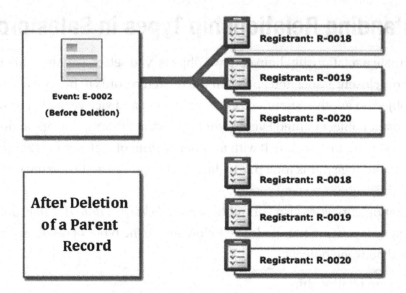

Figure 2-8. *An example of a lookup relationship*

For example, suppose there is a lookup relationship between the Event custom object and the Registrant custom object in which Event acts as the parent object and Registrant is a child object. If someone deletes the Event record, all related Registrant records remain in the system without the parent (see Figure 2-9).

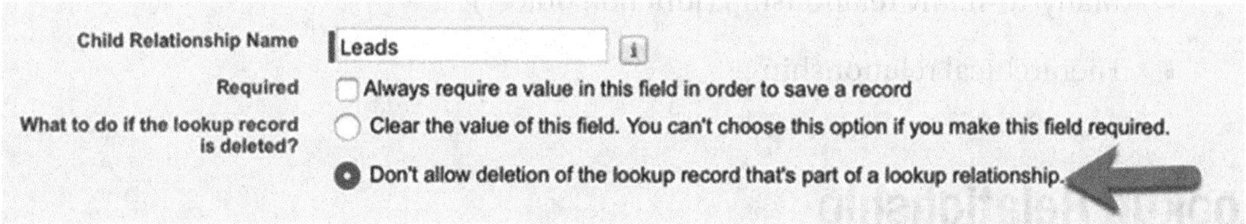

Child Relationship Name	Leads ℹ
Required	☐ Always require a value in this field in order to save a record
What to do if the lookup record is deleted?	○ Clear the value of this field. You can't choose this option if you make this field required.
	◉ Don't allow deletion of the lookup record that's part of a lookup relationship. ⬅

Figure 2-9. *Settings available for a lookup relationship*

Please study Figure 2-9 carefully. When you do, you should notice that if you select the "Don't allow deletion of the lookup record that's part of a lookup relationship." check box, then it is not possible to delete a parent record that has child records! However, in such a scenario, *you could delete the child record without any issue*!

Self-Relationship

Self-relationship is a type of lookup relationship. You can use the lookup relationship to create a self-relationship between objects. You can have a maximum of 40 lookup relationships in an object. For example, a Case record can have a Parent Case record, as shown in Figure 2-10.

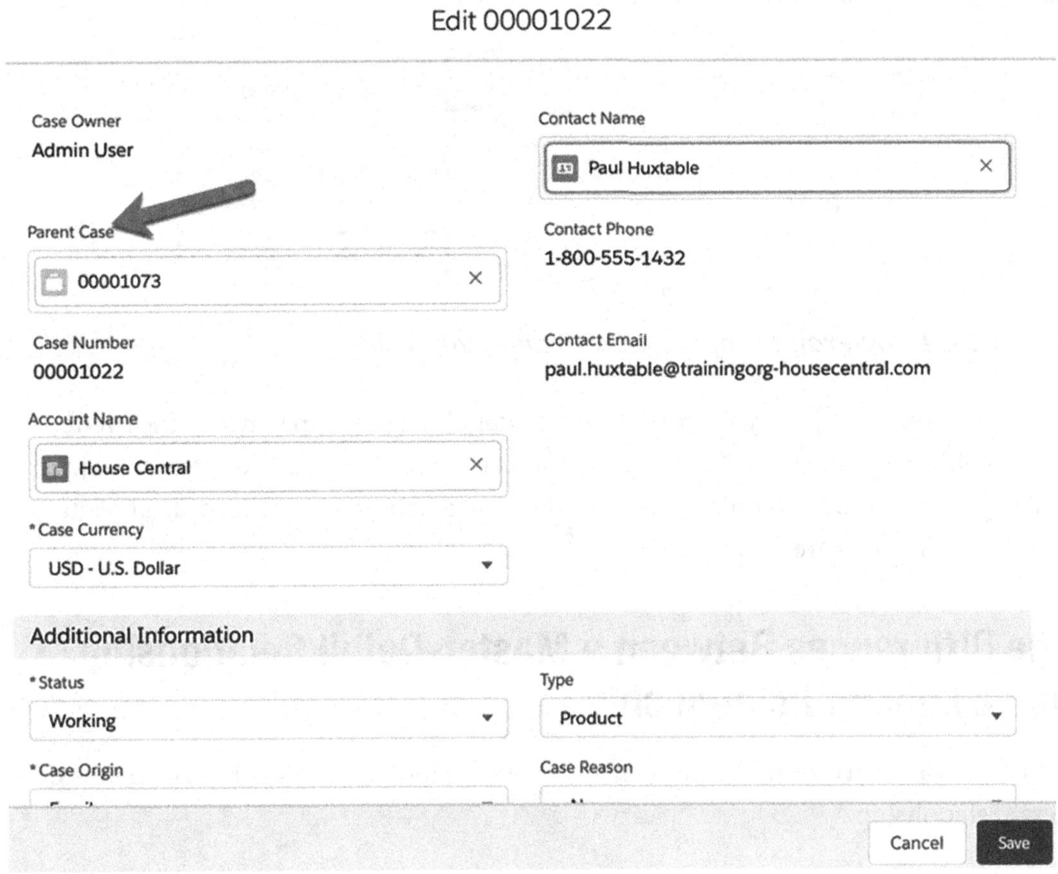

Figure 2-10. An example of a self-relationship

Master-Detail Relationship

Master-detail is a strongly connected relationship between Salesforce objects. This means that if someone deletes the parent record, the child's records are also deleted. In this type of relationship, the parent record controls the accessibility of its child records. It also means that if users have access to a parent record, they also have access to the related child records (see Figure 2-11).

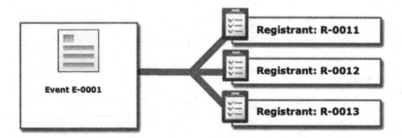

Figure 2-11. *An example of a master-detail relationship*

For example, suppose you create a master-detail relationship between the Event custom object and the Registrant custom object, where Event acts as a parent object and Registrant is a child object. Then, if someone deletes an Event record, all related Registrant records are also deleted.

The Differences Between a Master-Detail Relationship and a Lookup Relationship

Table 2-2 is an overview of the differences between a lookup relationship and a master-detail relationship.

Table 2-2. *Lookup Relationship vs. Master-Detail Relationship*

Lookup Relationship	Master-Detail Relationship
It is loosely connected.	It is strongly connected.
A roll-up summary field cannot be created.	A roll-up summary field can be created.
A parent record is not required (it's optional) when creating a child record.	A parent record is always required to create a child record.
Lookup fields are not required on the page layout of the detail record.	The `Master-Detail` field is always required on the page layout of the detail record.
A standard object record can be on the detail side of a custom object record.	A standard object record cannot be a child or on the detail side of the relationship.
The parent does not control ownership of child records.	The parent controls ownership of the child's records. The `Owner` field is not available in the child record in a master-detail relationship.
You can have a child record without a parent.	You cannot have a child record without a parent.
You can have a maximum of 40 lookup relationships on an object.	You can have a maximum of two master-detail relationships on an object.

External Lookup Relationship

When you create an external object in Salesforce, you are introduced to two new lookup relationships: an external lookup relationship and an indirect lookup relationship. An external lookup relationship allows you to establish a relationship between a child standard, custom, or external object and an external parent object with data stored in an external data source.

Indirect Lookup Relationship

An indirect lookup relationship allows you to establish a relationship between a child external object and a parent standard or custom object. You can only create an indirect lookup to an object that has a unique external ID field on the parent object that is used to match the records in this relationship. When creating an indirect lookup relationship field on an external object, you must specify the child object field and the parent object field to match and associate records in the relationship. For example, you can display a related list of payments from the Systems Applications Products (SAP) external record by matching external IDs on the `Account` object.

Many-to-Many Relationship

The many-to-many relationship in Salesforce allows you to associate a child record with multiple parents and vice versa with the help of an intermediate object. For example, a campaign is attached to multiple leads, and one lead may be associated with more than one campaign.

If you want to relate two objects—for example, `Account` and `Contact`—in such a manner that one account can have multiple contacts associated with it, you must use a many-to-many relationship. To establish a many-to-many relationship, you must use a third object known as a *junction object* (see Figure 2-12). Indeed, to establish a many-to-many relationship between `Account` and `Contact` objects, Salesforce offers a junction object known as `AccountContactRelation`.

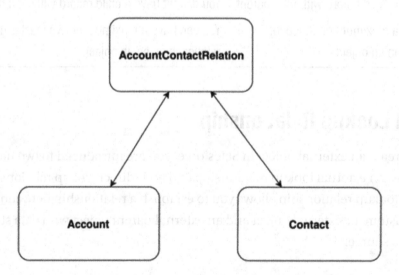

Figure 2-12. *An example of a many-to-many relationship*

Hierarchal Relationship

A hierarchical relationship is only available in the User object. With this type of relationship, you can create a hierarchy of users in an organization. For example, a user can have a reporting manager (custom hierarchical field, as shown in Figure 2-13), and her reporting manager may have another reporting manager, and so on until the CEO level.

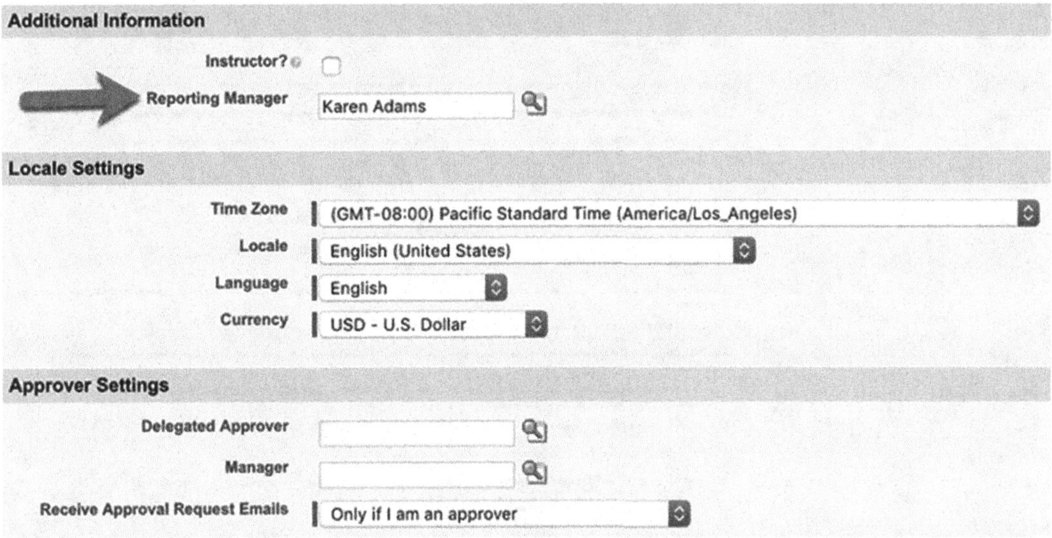

Figure 2-13. *An example of a hierarchical relationship*

Selecting the Appropriate Field Type

When you studied Schema Builder, you created a field. Now, let's take this topic further and look at how to select a field type.

As you now know, all objects in Salesforce have a predefined set of fields to store common business information, known as *standard fields*. It is possible to customize the standard field's label and help text; however, you cannot delete or rename the API of a standard field.

Sometimes, it is necessary to create a custom field instead of using a standard field. For example, to store a Social Security number, you need to display the last four digits to an end user like XXX-XX-1234. To achieve this, you create a custom field. Salesforce allows you to add custom fields to standard and custom objects to capture additional information required for your business. The best part is, if you create a custom field and then later find you no longer need it, you can delete it.

When creating a custom field, the first step is to select the field type, such as Email, Text, Number, Geolocation, and so on. These field types come with system-defined validation rules (see Figure 2-14).

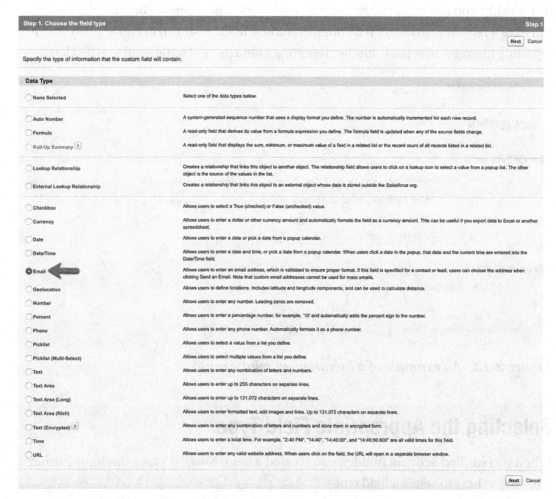

Figure 2-14. *Selecting an appropriate field type*

For example, if you select Email as the field type, users are allowed to enter an email address that is validated by the system to ensure the proper format is used. Some field types allow you to maintain data quality, such as Picklist, Picklist (Multi-Select), and Checkbox.

HANDS-ON EXERCISE

- Explore how many different field types are available when creating a custom field.

- Write down the properties of the Picklist, Checkbox, and Text (Encrypted) field types and notice the differences.

Because this is a straightforward exercise, an "answer" is not provided in the appendix.

Understanding Field Dependencies

To maintain data quality, Salesforce allows you to establish field dependencies between fields. Field dependency means the control value of one field is based on the value of another field. For example, if users decide to receive a newsletter, you can ask them to select the type of newsletter they would like to receive, as shown in Figure 2-15.

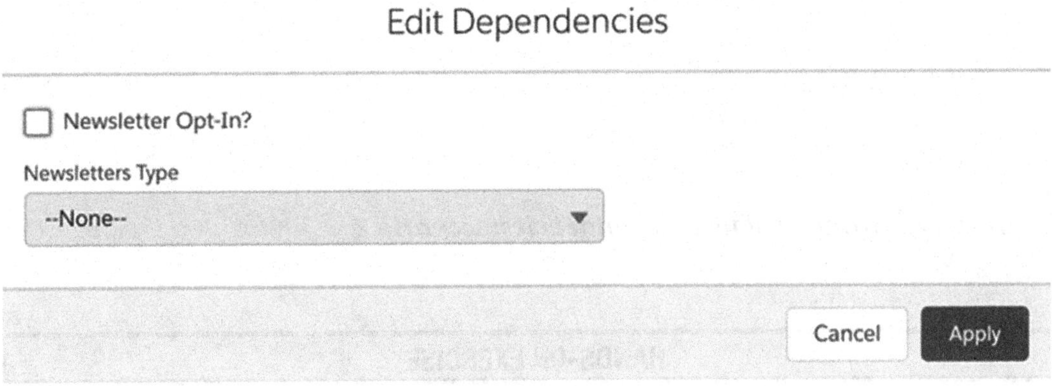

Figure 2-15. *How field dependencies can be used*

When you look at Figure 2-15 carefully, you might notice that the Newsletters Type field is Read Only because the Newsletter Opt-In? field is not yet selected.

Now let's select the Newsletter Opt-In? field and then select a newsletter type, as shown in Figure 2-16.

Edit Dependencies

☑ Newsletter Opt-In?

Newsletters Type

| Wellness Wire ▾ |

| Cancel | Apply |

Figure 2-16. *Example of field dependencies: scenario 1*

Let's take another scenario. If field dependencies are not in place, then users are able to select a newsletter type without opting in to receive a newsletter (see Figure 2-17). This doesn't make any sense, and such inconsistencies in the data also negatively impact data quality. It is important to understand the role of field dependencies and how they affect data quality and integrity. As a best practice, whenever possible, use field dependencies to improve data quality.

Figure 2-17. *Example of field dependencies: scenario 2*

HANDS-ON EXERCISE

- Create one check box field on the Lead object Newsletter Opt-In?.

- Create one more field (Newsletters Type) on the Lead object. The data type of the field should be Picklist and have the following values.

  - Wellness Wire

  - Nutrition

  - Women's Wellness

- Men's Health

- Becoming a Mother

- Senior Health

- Allergies

- Bipolar Illness

- Breast Cancer

Because this is a straightforward exercise, an "answer" is not provided in the appendix.

Setting up Field Dependencies

Now that we've studied field dependencies, it's time to set them up. Let's go back to our business scenario. Robin Guzman wants to understand the process of establishing field dependencies between the Newsletter Opt-In? and Newsletters Type fields. He performs the following steps.

1. He clicks Setup (gear icon) ➤ Setup Home ➤ Object Manager ➤ Lead ➤ Fields & Relationships.

2. He selects the Field Dependencies button, which redirects him to the Field Dependencies management page.

3. Robin navigates to the field dependencies-related list and clicks the New button, as shown in Figure 2-18.

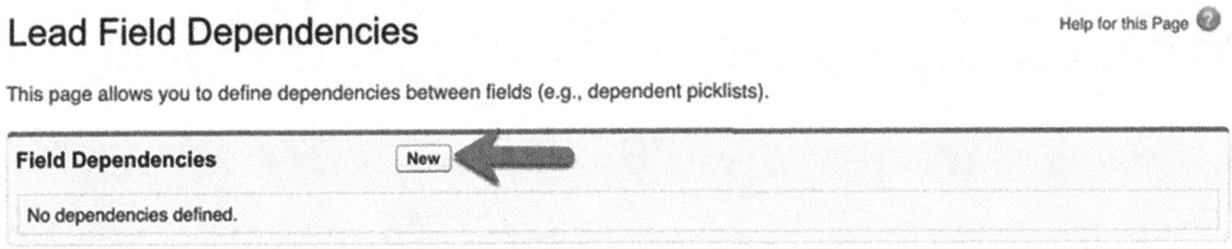

Figure 2-18. *First screen of the field dependencies setup process*

4. He selects Controlling Field and Dependent Field, as shown in Figure 2-19.

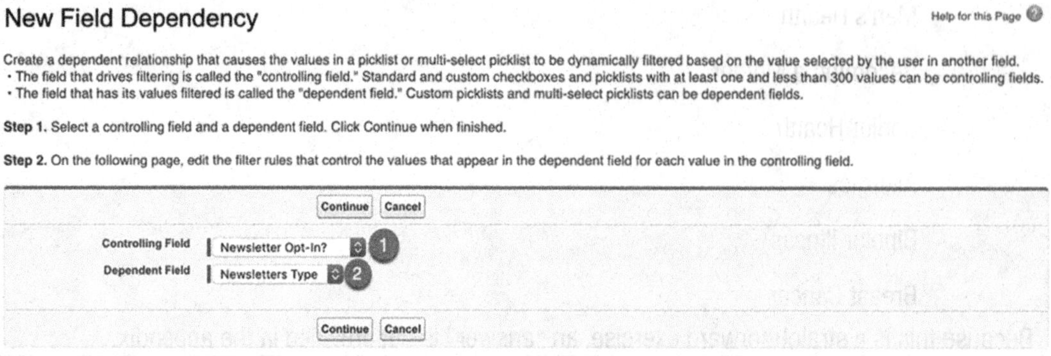

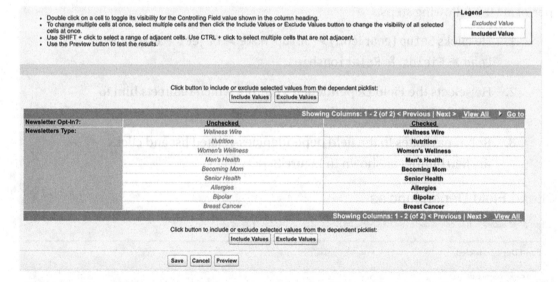

Figure 2-19. *The second screen of the field dependencies wizard allows the administrator to select* Controlling Field *and* Dependent Field

5. Robin then clicks the Continue button.

6. He selects the appropriate newsletter types in each column by double-clicking them (see Figure 2-20).

Figure 2-20. *The third screen of the field dependencies wizard allows the administrator to select values for the dependent picklist*

7. Finally, he clicks the Save button.

Tip   Check out the Salesforce documentation at `https://help.salesforce`
`.com/articleView?id=fields_dependent_field_considerations`
`.htm&type=5` to learn more about dependent fields.

Implications of Changing a Field's Type

By now, you should be clear on what a field type is, how field dependencies affect data quality, and how to set up field dependencies. If there is *any* confusion about these topics, reread the material and master the concepts. When you master them, you will almost be ready for your Platform App Builder exam!

Note   Review the Salesforce release notes to ensure you are aware of the latest developments on the platform.

This section refers to our business scenario to show how to change a field type. First, I must mention that, in most situations, *changing the data type of a custom field results in the loss of the field data.* List views based on the field will be deleted. In addition, changing a field type may affect assignment and escalation rules. As a best practice, don't change the field type; instead, create and use new fields. Only when a field doesn't have any data should you modify the field's data type. Before changing it, make sure to create a backup of your data, just in case you lose it. *Changing to* `Picklist (Multi-Select)` *from any other type results in lost data.* Now, let's rejoin Robin.

Robin has been praised by his manager for creating the `Newsletter Opt-In?` and `Newsletters Type` fields and for setting their field dependencies. Now, he is tasked to change the `Newsletters Type` field type from `Picklist` to `Picklist (Multi-Select)`. To do this, Robin performs the following steps.

1. He selects Setup (gear icon) ➤ `Setup Home` ➤ `Object Manager` ➤ `Lead` ➤ `Fields & Relationships`.

2. He clicks the `Edit` link available next to the `Newsletters Type` custom field, as shown in Figure 2-21.

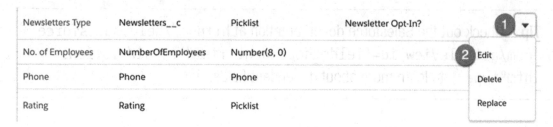

Newsletters Type	Newsletters__c	Picklist	Newsletter Opt-In?	1 ▼
No. of Employees	NumberOfEmployees	Number(8, 0)		2 Edit
Phone	Phone	Phone		Delete
Rating	Rating	Picklist		Replace

Figure 2-21. How to edit a field from the object manager

3.   He clicks the Change Field Type button, as shown in Figure 2-22.

Edit Lead Custom Field
Newsletters Type

Help for this Page

| Custom Field Definition Edit | Change Field Type | Promote to Global Value Set | Save | Cancel |

Field Information   ▌ = Required Information

Field Label	Newsletters Type	Data Type	Picklist
Field Name	Newsletters
Description	
Help Text	

Figure 2-22. How to change the field type for a custom field

4.   Robin selects the new data type: Picklist (Multi-Select).

5.   Then, he clicks the Next button.

6.   At this point, Robin can change the field label, name, and any other attributes.

7.   Finally, he clicks the Save button.

Tip   Check out the Salesforce documentation at https://help.salesforce
.com/articleView?id=notes_on_changing_custom_field_types
.htm&type=5 to learn more about changing custom field types.

Exploring External Objects

An external object is similar to a custom object. External objects are usually identified by the __x suffix. They allow you to bring data from external systems (data stored outside your Salesforce organization) to your Salesforce org without writing any code. Figure 2-23 depicts the process using Lightning Connect.

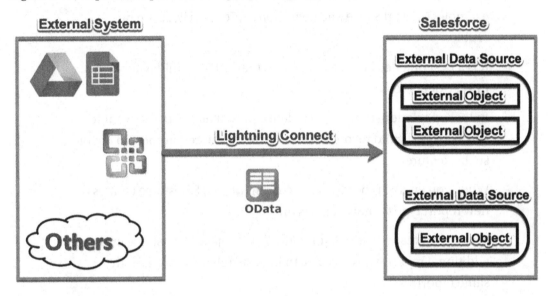

Figure 2-23. *How an external system and Salesforce are connected via Lightning Connect*

Each external object relies on an external data source definition, such as Lightning Connect or OData, to connect with an external system. You can connect each data table from an external system to an external object. Each of the external object fields maps to a table column in the external system.

Tip   To get hands-on experience using external objects, I highly recommend exploring the Trailhead module at https://trailhead.salesforce.com/ en/content/learn/modules/lightning_connect/lightning_connect_ integrate.

Points to Remember

- Schema Builder can't be used to export the org schema.

- The Geolocation field is not available through Schema Builder.

- Not all standard objects are available in Schema Builder. For example, AccountShare and OpportunityContactRole are not visible.

- It is a best practice not to create more than 10,000 child records in a master-detail relationship.

- In lookup relationships, if you delete a parent and you also want to delete related child records, reach out to Salesforce support to enable such a feature.

- When you enable reporting on a custom object, Salesforce creates a new report type to build reports on it.

- When you create relationships with other objects, Salesforce creates additional report types so you can include related records in the same report.

- You can define a custom Picklist field as a Controlling or a Dependent field.

- The standard Picklist field must be a Controlling field; it can never be a Dependent field.

- It is not possible to change field types for standard fields.

- It is not possible to select Picklist (Multi-Select) as a Controlling field.

- It is not possible to select Checkbox as a Dependent field.

- It is not possible to change the data type of a standard field.

- One Salesforce org can have 100 external objects. External objects do not count against the number of custom object limits.

Hands-on Exercises

The following exercises give you more practice with the platform, which ultimately helps you gain mastery of the platform and helps you prepare for the certification examination. Remember, these are hands-on exercises, and you can find the answers in the appendix at the back of the book, but try to implement the exercises in your Salesforce org.

1. Use Schema Builder to learn about the data model of the following objects.

    a. Product, Price Book, and Price Book Entry

    b. Opportunity and Opportunity Product

    c. Quote and Quote Line Item

2. Add the custom field Next Meeting Date to the Opportunity object using Schema Builder to store the next meeting date. Set the field-level security (Read/Write) for the following standard profiles.

    a. System administrator

    b. Contract manager

    c. Marketing user

3. Dennis Williams is a system administrator at GoC. He is tasked with creating a field to store Social Security numbers. He also needs to mask all the characters so no one can see the data behind the field. Which field types should he use?

4. Dennis is required to create one field in the Contact object to store client photographs. Which field type should he use?

5. Dennis is tasked with creating a field that allows users to store customer geolocation, including latitude and longitude. Which field type should he use?

6. Denise wants to implement opportunity management at GoC, but he is a bit confused by one of the requirements. Because you now have a better understanding of field types, please help him select the appropriate field type to display the Account Site field value in the Opportunity record.

In addition, Dennis needs the Account Site field to show the latest value. This means that if the value of the Account Site field is changed from Mumbai to Dallas, then the Account Site field value should reflect Dallas.

7. Create two custom picklist fields per the following requirements.

   a. Country (Picklist Multi-Select): India, United States, Japan, China, Canada, the Netherlands, United Kingdom, Spain, Mexico, Brazil, Peru, Colombia, and Greece. Sort these values in alphabetical order.

   b. Business Region (Picklist): APAC, EMEA, NA, and LATAM. Sort these values in alphabetical order.

   c. Set up field dependencies between the Business Region and Country fields based on the following table.

Business Region	Country
APAC	India, Japan, China
EMEA	Spain, the Netherlands, Greece, the United Kingdom
NA	United States, Canada
LATAM	Mexico, Brazil, Peru, Colombia

8. Help Dennis select the appropriate relationship field to connect the Consumer (parent) and License (child) custom objects. Later, he plans to create a roll-up summary field on the parent object.

9. Dennis has been given the task of establishing a relationship between the Meetup__c and Participants__c objects. He needs to achieve the following capabilities.

   a. When a user deletes the Meetup record, they get an error message if there are child Participant records associated with it.

   b. Dennis needs to make sure the parent lookup field is marked "required" on the child record. Which field type should he use?

10. Create two custom objects: Meetup and Participants. Here are
     the fields for both objects.

     a. Meetup object: Meetup Start Date/Time, Meetup End Date/Time,
         Location Details, Description, and Meetup Name. Meetup Name should
         be an autonumbered field.

     b. Participants object: First Name, Last Name, Email, Date of Birth,
         Phone, Mailing Address, Annual Income, and the values for status drop-
         down are Yes and No.

     Now, establish a lookup relationship between these two objects.
     Insert a few Participant records without associating them with
     a Meetup record. Change the relationship type from lookup to
     master detail.

11. Keeping the previous exercise in mind, create a field in the
     Meetup record to show the number of people who answered yes
     while RSVPing.

Summary

This chapter examined the basics of metadata and why we need it, followed by an
in-depth look at Schema Builder. It also studied various relationship types available in
Salesforce. It looked at field types, field dependencies, and implications of changing field
types. Finally, it examined external objects and their use cases. The next chapter takes an
in-depth look at platform security and settings.

CHAPTER 3

Platform Security

Abstract

Chapter 2 examined Salesforce data modeling, metadata, and Schema Builder. It studied the different types of relationships in Salesforce, used real-world examples of how to select field types for a field, and studied the implications of changing a field type.

This chapter consists of two main parts. The first part covers the following.

- Organization-wide default (OWD)

- Role hierarchies

- Record sharing

- Profiles

- Permission Set

- Custom permission

The second part of this chapter looks at how to set up security at the object and field levels.

OWD: A Baseline Setting for Objects

When I started learning Salesforce in 2012, the following questions haunted me.

- What is an *organization-wide default*, also known as OWD?

- How does OWD affect Salesforce record accessibility?

- Who can set up OWD?

- What are the key considerations for setting up OWD?

R. Gupta, *Salesforce Platform App Builder Certification Companion*, Certification Study Companion Series

By the end of this section, you'll know the answers to these questions. Each one is explored in detail, so let's get started.

Have you ever wondered the following?

- Why am I able to view and/or edit records owned by some users but not by others?

- Why am I not able to view and/or edit records that I do not own?

- Why am I not able to view and/or edit the records that I own?

Look no further than your organization's OWD settings! Let's decrypt OWD and get to the bottom of this.

OWD is a security design model. It is a baseline setting for objects in a Salesforce org that determines default record access for all users and for all records within each object!

It is one of the simplest *and* one of the most complicated concepts. Yes, an oxymoron indeed! So, let's explore it through the example of Pamela Kline, a Salesforce administrator at GoC.

- Pamela resides at 1622 Davidson Street, Alpharetta. No outsiders— except her friends and family—are allowed on the premises. This means it is private property. Another example is an office space. If an office space is marked *private*, people entering the space without permission could be punished or even jailed for trespassing. A Private model enables owners of the property to prohibit access to outsiders.

- On December 24, Pamela went to IKEA to buy a new couch. There, she met Julia Roberts, a sales manager. Julia helped Pamela find the perfect couch. IKEA is a *public* place, so Pamela can access the entire store, but she is not allowed to change any of the store's settings. Another good example is a museum. People can visit, explore, and learn at museums, but they cannot dictate where a painting or an artifact can be placed. These examples are equivalent to a Public Read Only model in Salesforce, in which users can view a record owned by others, but they do not have permission to make any changes to the record.

- Pamela is eager to learn new stuff on the Internet. Munira Majmundar, Pamela's neighbor, introduces her to Wikipedia. Wikipedia is a free online encyclopedia created and managed by volunteers across the globe. Anyone can update a Wikipedia page if they find something inaccurate. This is equivalent to a Public Read/ Write model in Salesforce.

When you comb through these examples carefully, one thing should stand out: *the permission level in each of the three scenarios is different*—namely, Private, Public Read Only, and Public Read/Write. Figure 3-1 visualizes the concept.

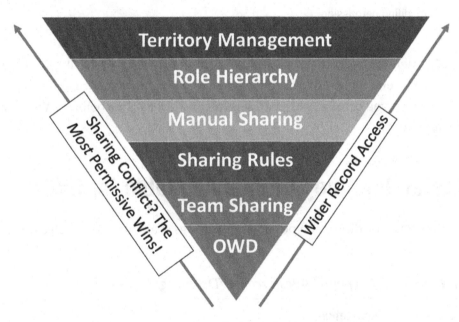

Figure 3-1. *Controlling data access with the Salesforce platform*

Table 3-1 is just a table until you realize that it comprises real-life examples mirroring Salesforce's OWD terminology!

Table 3-1. *Representation of Real-life Examples with Respect to Salesforce OWD*

Places	Permission Levels	Actions One Can Perform	Salesforce-Equivalent OWD
Pamela's house	Private property	None (except for Pamela and her friends and family)	Private
IKEA	Open to the public, with read permission	View	Public Read Only
Wikipedia	Open to the public, with modified permission	View/edit	Public Read/Write

Figure 3-1 demonstrates major pillars that control record-level sharing among different sets of users, where OWD is the base-level setting for standard and custom objects. Therefore, you cannot restrict a user's record-level access below OWD. It is the most restrictive of all.

Understanding the Settings Available for OWD

Table 3-2 describes the different types of OWD settings available within Salesforce.

Table 3-2. *Different Types of Salesforce OWD Settings*

OWD Settings	Explanation
Private	When the OWD of an object is set to Private, the record is visible to the owner. Create-Read-Update-Delete (CRUD) access is required to perform CRUD actions, which is discussed later in this chapter.
	If owners are assigned a role and the Grant Access Using Hierarchies check box is checked, then the owners have complete access (read, edit, delete, and share) to records they own and all the records owned by users below in the role hierarchy. Note: *The Grant Access Using Hierarchies feature is checked by default on standard objects and cannot be unchecked.*

(continued)

Table 3-2. (*continued*)

OWD Settings	Explanation
Public Read Only	When the OWD of an object is set to Public Read Only, it allows users to view all records of an object. CRUD access is required to perform CRUD actions. If owners are assigned a role and the `Grant Access Using Hierarchies` check box is checked, then the owners have complete access (read, edit, delete, and share) to records they own and all the records owned by users below in the role hierarchy. This permission allows users to report on records to which they have access.
Public Read/Write	When the OWD of an object is set to Public Read/Write, users can view and edit all records of an object. CRUD access is required to perform CRUD actions. In this case, if the `Grant Access Using Hierarchies` check box is checked, then all users have complete access (read, edit, and delete) to the records they own and all the records owned by users below them in the role hierarchy. This permission allows users to report on all records.
Controlled by Parent	This option is used if you want to allow users to view the related (child) records only when they have access to the parent record. CRUD access is required to perform CRUD actions.
Public Read/Write/ Transfer	This option is used if you want to allow users to view, edit, and transfer all records. This setting is only available for `Case` and `Lead` objects. This permission allows users to report on all records.
Public Full Access	This option is used if you want to allow users to view, edit, delete, and transfer all records. This setting is only available for the `Campaign` object. This permission allows users to report on all records.
Use (available for price book)	This option is used if you want to allow users to view the price book and associated products. This setting allows them to use the price book on an opportunity.
View Only (available for price book)	This option is used if you want to allow users to view the price book and associated products but don't want to give them the ability to use the price book on an opportunity.
No Access (available for price book)	With this option, users with Manage Price Book permission can access price books for maintenance.

Predefined OWD for Objects

When you create a new Salesforce org, it comes with OWD settings for standard and custom objects. Salesforce gives you the ability to modify them per your business needs. You can view your org's default OWD settings by navigating as follows: Setup (gear icon) ➤ Setup ➤ SETTINGS ➤ Security ➤ ➤ Sharing Settings. The predefined OWD access for standard and custom objects is shown in Table 3-3.

Table 3-3. *Predefined OWD Access for Standard and Custom Objects*

Object	Default Access
Account	Public Read/Write
Activity	Private
Asset	Controlled by Parent
Campaign	Public Full Access
Campaign Member	Controlled by Parent
Case	Public Read/Write Transfer
Contact	Controlled by Parent
Contract	Public Read/Write
Custom Object	Public Read/Write
Lead	Public Read/Write Transfer
Opportunity	Public Read Only
Order	Controlled by Parent
Price Book	Use
Users	Public Read Only, and Private for external users

The Importance of Role Hierarchy

Role hierarchy has a major impact on record sharing in Salesforce. Therefore, defining the hierarchy correctly for your org is a critical design consideration.

The role hierarchy may or may not mirror your company's hierarchy. Depending on your business needs, you can create users with or without assigning them a role. Similarly, a role can have one or more than one user assigned to it.

The role hierarchy works in conjunction with OWD. When studying various OWD settings, you may have noticed that if an owner has a role and the Grant Access Using Hierarchies check box is checked, then users have complete access (read, edit, delete, and share) to records they own and to the records owned by users below them in the role hierarchy. Remember that OWD determines access to objects, but it is the role hierarchy that grants users access to records they own and records owned by users below them in the role hierarchy.

Use Case 1

Pamela Kline is working as a system administrator at GoC. She is currently implementing campaign management. She understands how objects within a campaign connect with each other. Pamela is given the following requirements.

- Inside sales team members should not be able to view leads owned by other inside sales team members.

- The inside sales manager, however, should be able to view, edit, and share access to leads with any users assigned to inside sales team members.

Figure 3-2 shows GoC's current organizational chart.

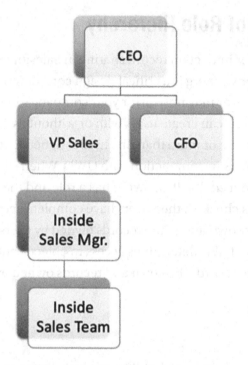

Figure 3-2. *An abbreviated functional organizational structure of GoC*

Before developing any solution, think of OWD because it is the *base-level setting* that restricts object-level access in Salesforce. For Pamela to meet her requirements, she must set OWD for the Lead object to Private and Grant Access Using Hierarchies to True.

Pamela performs the following steps using OWD.

1. She clicks Setup (gear icon) ➤ Setup ➤ SETTINGS > Security ➤ Sharing Settings ➤ Edit.

2. Pamela navigates to the OWD settings for the Lead object and sets Default Internal Access to Private.

3. If you look at Figure 3-3 carefully, the Grant Access Using Hierarchies field is *selected by default,* and users are not allowed to change this setting. However, on custom objects, you can select this option. By granting access, the inside sales manager can access Lead records assigned to the inside sales team.

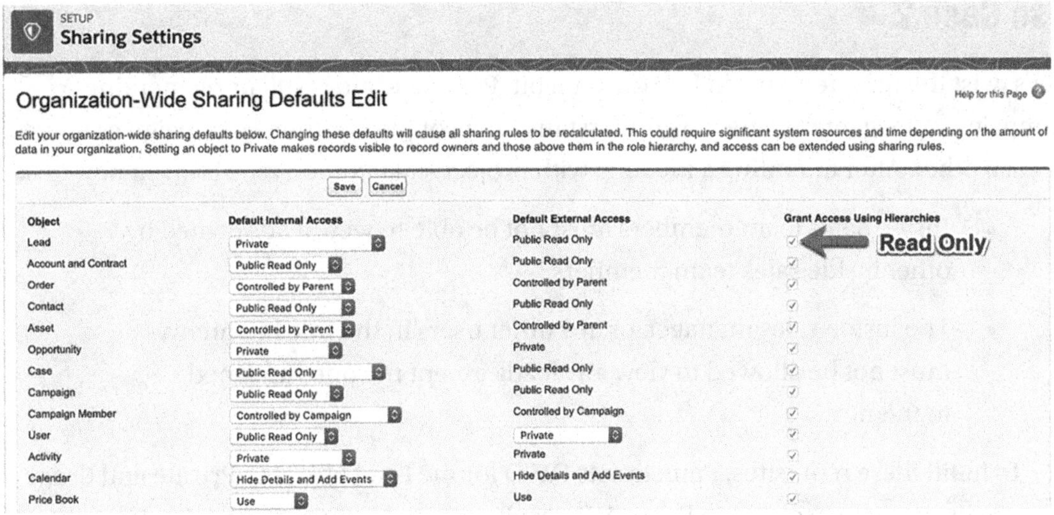

Figure 3-3. OWD settings

4.   When done, Pamela clicks the Save button.

Table 3-4 explains internal and external access for organization-wide settings.

Table 3-4. *Differences in Internal and External Access*

Access	Explanation
Default internal access	Internal access is for internal user license types.
Default external access	External users include the following licenses. • Guest users • Chatter external users • Community users • Customer portal users • High-volume portal users • Partner portal users • Service Cloud portal users • Authenticated website users

Use Case 2

Let's twist the requirements in Use Case 1 a bit. Pamela Kline is still implementing campaign management. She now understands how objects within a campaign connect to each other. After attending a meeting with project stakeholders, she is given new tasks.

- Inside Sales team members must not be able to view leads owned by other inside sales team members.

- The inside sales manager, or any other users in the role hierarchy, must not be allowed to view any leads except the ones assigned to them.

To fulfill these requisites, Pamela sets OWD for the Lead object to Private and Grant Access Using Hierarchies to False. As a result, users who do not own a lead are not able to see it.

Oh! You caught the Herculean error in Pamela's solution. You realized that Pamela *cannot set* Grant Access Using Hierarchies to *False* for the Lead object because the Lead object is a standard object, and therefore, Grant Access Using Hierarchies is checked *by default, and users are not allowed to change it.* Bravo!

Because it is not possible to change Grant Access Using Hierarchies on a standard object, as you correctly noted, Pamela must create a workaround. As a result, Pamela considers the following options.

1. Create a custom object to store leads—for example, Prospect__c.

   a. Set custom object Prospect__c OWD to Private.

   b. Set Grant Access Using Hierarchies to False.

2. Use a standard Lead object.

   a. Set Lead object OWD to Private.

   b. Set Grant Access Using Hierarchies to True (because you can't change it).

   c. Use Visualforce Page or Lightning Web Components as the main interface.

   d. Behind the scenes, write custom logic to display the record based on the owner!

These possible workarounds demonstrate how a single setting in Salesforce—in this case, Grant Access Using Hierarchies—can pose challenges if you fail to understand their implications.

Setting up Role Hierarchies

Whenever users are created, as a best practice, the system administrator should always assign a role to them. If no role is assigned, users are only able to view/access records assigned to them, assuming OWD is set to Private. Note that users can only be assigned a role at the system level, not the object level.

Please make sure you read and reread the previous section on the importance of role hierarchies so you thoroughly understand the significance a role plays in Salesforce with regard to enabling users to access and share records they own or do not own.

It is worth repeating: *only* if users are assigned a role can the system administrator grant them read, edit, delete, and share access to records owned by them or owned by users below them in the role hierarchy. For instance, even if two users are at the same level—such as the chief operating officer (COO) and the chief information officer (CIO)—they are not able to access each other's records until they have a role assigned to them, assuming that OWD for the object is not Public Read Only or Public Read/Write.

Recall that the role hierarchy works in conjunction with OWD—meaning, whether the role hierarchy affects access to a record depends on the OWD value set for the object. If OWD for an object is Public Read Only, then every user in the organization would be able to view the records within the object. Simple—assuming they have read access via profiles.

Take a minute to review GoC's organizational chart, as shown in Figure 3-4.

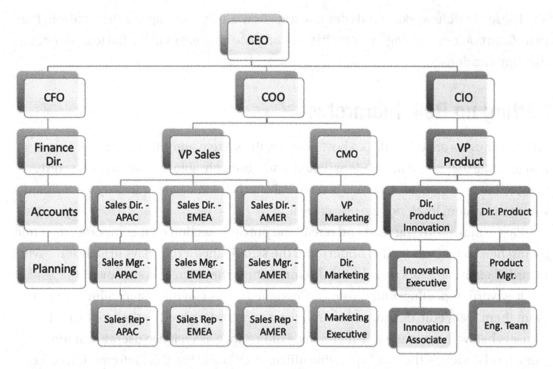

Figure 3-4. *GoC organizational chart*

Let's get back to Pamela. She hasn't had an opportunity to set up a role hierarchy in Salesforce, but she is keen to do it. To start, she wants to set up the CEO's role.

Before she begins, she relies on her best practice know-how to delete all existing roles (default roles that come with a new Salesforce org) before creating a new set of role hierarchies. Then, Pamela performs the following steps to create the CEO's role hierarchy.

1. She clicks Setup (gear icon) ➤ Setup ➤ ADMINISTRATION ➤ Users ➤ Roles.

2. She clicks Add Role below the company name, as shown in Figure 3-5.

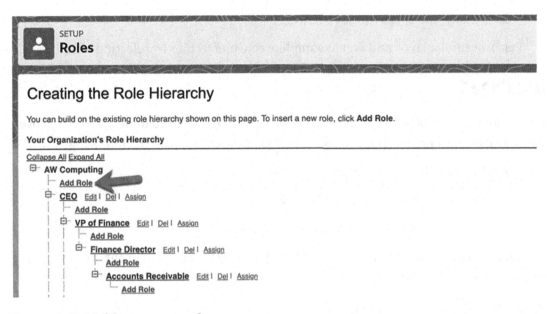

Figure 3-5. *Adding a new role*

3. She enters values for Label and Role Name and makes sure to select an option in This role reports to. Pamela selects the company name.

4. Then, she selects the CEO's access level to Contact, Opportunity, and Case, as shown in Figure 3-6.

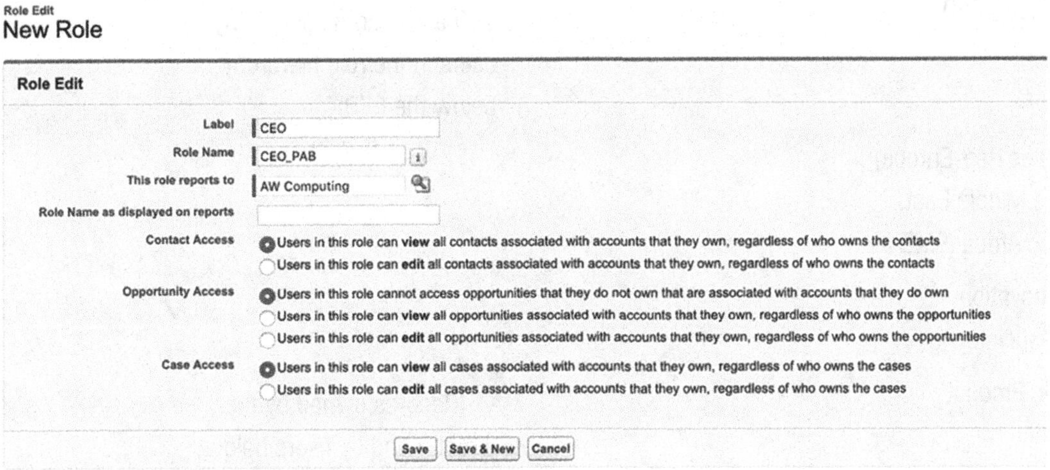

Figure 3-6. *Defining access level*

5. Finally, she clicks the Save button.

Perform similar steps and create complete role hierarchies by referring to Figure 3-5.

Use Case 1

Before going ahead, know that you'll need to refer to Figure 3-4 to understand these use cases. Let's look at how record access is granted to users based on the following.

- Custom object: Prospect__c

- Organization-wide setting: Private

- Grant Access Using Hierarchies: True

Table 3-5 shows what happens when OWD is set to Private, and Grant Access Using Hierarchies is set to True.

Table 3-5. *Record Access for Use Case 1*

Role	Access All Records	Access All Records Owned by Users Assigned to a Role	Access Records: Self-Owned and Those Owned by Users Below in the Role Hierarchy	Access Records: Self-Owned Records Only
CEO		✓		
Chief Financial Officer (CFO)			✓ (Records owned by the CFO and records owned by users in the role hierarchy below the CFO)	
Sales Rep-Europe, the Middle East, and Africa (EMEA)				✓
Innovation Associate				✓
Dir. Product			✓ (Records owned by the director and by users below in the role hierarchy)	
Users with no role				✓

In Table 3-5, access is granted as follows.

- The CEO gets complete access (read, edit, delete, and share) to all records in the organization that have an assigned user. As a result, if a role is not assigned to a user, then neither the CEO nor anyone else in the organization can see records owned by that user.

- The CFO and CIO are not able to access each other's records even though they are at the same level.

- The CFO gets complete access (read, edit, delete, and share) to records owned by her and those owned by users in the Finance Dir, Accounts, and Planning roles.

- Sales Rep-EMEA and Innovation Associate can see only those records assigned/owned by them.

- Dir. Product gets complete access (read, edit, delete, and share) to records owned by him and those owned by users in the Product Mgr. and Eng. Team roles.

Use Case 2

Now, let's tweak the scenario and change Grant Access Using Hierarchies to False (Table 3-6). Then, let's examine how record access is granted to users based on the following.

- Custom object: Prospect__c

- Organization-wide setting: Private

- Grant Access Using Hierarchies: False

Table 3-6. *Record Access for Use Case 2*

Role	Access All Records	Access All Records Owned by Users Assigned to a Role	Access Records: Self-Owned and Those Owned by Users Below in the Role Hierarchy	Access Records: Self-Owned Records Only
CEO				✓
CFO				✓
Sales Rep-EMEA				✓
Innovation Associate				✓
Dir. Product				✓
Users with no role				✓

It's as simple as that! When `Grant Access Using Hierarchies` is set to False, users only see those records they own. Period.

Use Case 3

Let's tweak the scenario again. This time, let's change OWD to Public Read Only and look at how record access is granted to users based on the following (Table 3-7).

- Custom object: `Prospect__c`

- Organization-wide setting: Public Read Only

- `Grant Access Using Hierarchies`: True

Table 3-7. *Record Access for Use Case 3*

Role	Access All Records	Access All Records Owned by Users Assigned to a Role	Access Records: Self-Owned and Those Owned by Users Below in the Role Hierarchy	Access Records: Self-Owned Records Only
CEO	✓			
CFO	✓			
Sales Rep-EMEA	✓			
Innovation Associate	✓			
Dir. Product	✓			
Users with no role	✓			

Because OWD is the baseline setting, if it is set to Public Read Only, all users can see all records regardless of whether they are assigned a role.

Use Case 4

Let's look at another scenario and how record view, edit, delete, and share capabilities work based on the following (Table 3-8).

- Custom object: Prospect__c

- Organization-wide setting: Private

- Grant Access Using Hierarchies: True

Table 3-8. Record Access for Use Case 4

Role	Read	Edit	Delete	Share
CEO	Records CEO owns and those owned by users below the CEO in the role hierarchy	Records CEO owns and those owned by users below the CEO in the role hierarchy	Records CEO owns and those owned by users below CEO in the role hierarchy	Records CEO owns and those owned by users below CEO in the role hierarchy
CFO	Records CFO owns and those owned by users in the Finance Dir, Accounts, and Planning roles	Records CFO owns and those owned by users in the Finance Dir, Accounts, and Planning roles	Records CFO owns and those owned by users in the Finance Dir, Accounts, and Planning roles	Records CFO owns and those owned by users in the Finance Dir, Accounts, and Planning roles
Sales Rep-EMEA	Only records Sales Rep-EMEA owns	Only records Sales Rep-EMEA owns	Only records Sales Rep-EMEA owns	Only records Sales Rep-EMEA owns
Innovation Associate	Only records Innovation Associate owns	Only records Innovation Associate owns	Only records Innovation Associate owns	Only records Innovation Associate owns
Dir. Product	Records Dir. Product owns and those owned by users in the Product Mgr. and Eng. Team roles	Records Dir. Product owns and those owned by users in the Product Mgr. and Eng. Team roles	Records Dir. Product owns and those owned by users in the Product Mgr. and Eng. Team roles	Records Dir. Product owns and those owned by users in the Product Mgr. and Eng. Team roles
Users with no role	Only records they own	Only records they own	Only records they own	Only records they own

Because OWD is the baseline setting, when it is set to Private, users are able to access records they own and those owned by users below them in the role hierarchy.

Use Case 5

In the next scenario, let's look at how record view, edit, delete, and share capabilities work based on the following (Table 3-9).

- Custom object: Prospect__c
- Organization-wide setting: Public Read Only
- Grant Access Using Hierarchies: True

Table 3-9. *Record Access for Use Case 5*

Role	Read	Edit	Delete	Share
CEO	All records	Records CEO owns and those owned by users below in the role hierarchy	Records CEO owns and those owned by users below in the role hierarchy	Records CEO owns and those owned by users below in the role hierarchy
CFO	All records	Records CFO owns and those owned by users in the Finance Dir, Accounts, and Planning roles	Records CFO owns and those owned by users in the Finance Dir, Accounts, and Planning roles	Records CFO owns and those owned by users in the Finance Dir, Accounts, and Planning roles
Sales Rep-EMEA	All records	Only records Sales Rep-EMEA owns	Only records Sales Rep-EMEA owns	Only records Sales Rep-EMEA owns
Innovation Associate	All records	Only records Innovation Associate owns	Only records Innovation Associate owns	Only records Innovation Associate owns
Dir. Product	All records	Records Dir. Product owns and those owned by users in the Product Mgr. and Eng. Team roles	Records Dir. Product owns and those owned by users in the Product Mgr. and Eng. Team roles	Records Dir. Product owns and those owned by users in the Product Mgr. and Eng. Team roles
Users with no role	All records	Only records they own	Only records they own	Only records they own

When OWD is Public Read Only and Grant Access Using Hierarchies is True, then, regardless of whether a role hierarchy is used in an org, all users can view all records (assuming they have Read access on the object via their profile). Furthermore, users can edit, delete, and share only those records they own or are owned by users below them in the role hierarchy.

Use Case 6

Let's look at another scenario and how record view, edit, delete, and share capabilities work (Table 3-10) with the following parameters.

- Custom object: Prospect__c

- Organization-wide setting: Public Read/Write

- Grant Access Using Hierarchies: True

Table 3-10. *Record Access for Use Case 6*

Role	Read	Edit	Delete	Share
CEO	All records	All records	Records CEO owns and records owned by users below in the role hierarchy	Records CEO owns and records owned by users below in the role hierarchy
CFO	All records	All records	Records CFO owns and records owned by users in the Finance Dir, Accounts, and Planning roles, and below in the role hierarchy	Records CFO owns and records owned by users in the Finance Dir, Accounts, and Planning roles, and below in the role hierarchy
Sales Rep-EMEA	All records	All records	Only records Sales Rep-EMEA owns	Only records Sales Rep-EMEA owns
Innovation Associate	All records	All records	Only records Innovation Associate owns	Only records Innovation Associate owns
Dir. Product	All records	All records	Records Dir. Product owns and records owned by users in the Product Mgr. and Engineering Team roles and below in the role hierarchy	Records Dir. Product owns and records owned by users in the Product Mgr. and Engineering Team roles and below in the role hierarchy
Users with no role	All records	All records	Only records they own	Only records they own

As shown in Table 3-10, when OWD is set to Public Read/Write and, because it is a baseline setting, even though users may not be below in the role hierarchy or may not have a role assigned to them, they are still able to read and edit all records.

Use Case 7

Let's look at another scenario and how record view, edit, delete, and share capabilities work (Table 3-11) with the following parameters.

- Custom object: Prospect__c

- Organization-wide setting: Public Read/Write

- Grant Access Using Hierarchies: False

Table 3-11. *Record Access for Use Case 7*

Role	Read	Edit	Delete	Share
CEO	All records	All records	Only records the CEO owns	Only records the CEO owns
CFO	All records	All records	Only records the CFO owns	Only records the CFO owns
Sales Rep-EMEA	All records	All records	Only records Sales Rep-EMEA owns	Only records Sales Rep-EMEA owns
Innovation Associate	All records	All records	Only records Innovation Associate owns	Only records Innovation Associate owns
Dir. Product	All records	All records	Only records Dir. Product owns	Only records Dir. Product owns
Users with no Role	All records	All records	Only records they own	Only records they own

In this scenario, OWD is Public Read/Write, but Grant Access Using Hierarchies is set to False. As a result, users are not able to delete or share records owned by users below them in the role hierarchy, assuming they have CRUD access to the object via profile.

I hope these use cases help you get a grip on the concepts of role hierarchy and OWD. If yes, awesome! You are making good progress! If you are still in doubt, no worries! Just reread and ponder these settings; try to visualize different scenarios. Later, make sure you perform a series of tests in your developer org.

Record-Sharing Capabilities

So far, we've looked at record accessibility based on role hierarchy and OWD. Sometimes, you may need to share records with users who are across the role hierarchy, *not below*. The following are a few examples of this.

- The COO wants to access all records owned by the CFO. They are both at the same level in terms of the role hierarchy. In this case, sharing needs to take place across and not below.

- The CIO wants to share a few records owned by the CIO with the chief marketing officer (CMO).

- The company wants to share all records owned by Sales Dir. APAC with Sales Dir. EMEA.

Sharing rules are used to open record access to groups of users, roles, or roles and subordinates, notwithstanding the OWD setting. The sharing rule can't be used to restrict record access. Salesforce has the following types of sharing rules.

- **Manual sharing**: A Sharing button is enabled on the record detail page if OWD is set to Private or Public Read Only for any object. The record owners, or users higher in the role hierarchy, can share records with other users on a one-off basis.

- **Criteria-based sharing**: This rule allows system administrators to write a rule based on field values in a record. This is very helpful when you want to share a particular type of record with someone— for example, sharing all leads for Mumbai with Sales Rep-Asia–Pacific (APAC). You can have a maximum of 50 criteria-based sharing rules per object.

- **Owner-based sharing**: This rule allows system administrators to write a rule based on the owner of a record—for example, share all leads owned by users in the Sales Rep-EMEA role with users in the Sales Rep–North, Central, and South America (AMER) roles.

- **Apex-managed sharing**: This rule gives you the flexibility to handle complex business scenarios using Apex. For example, you have a field on the Lead object known as Potential Owner (User lookup). When this field is populated, you want to share the Lead record with the potential owner. This kind of scenario is handled easily through the Apex-managed sharing rule. You can either write Apex Trigger or Flow with Process Builder to handle this type of scenario. To access sharing objects programmatically, you must use the shared object associated with the standard or custom object you want to share.

Manual Sharing: Share Records on a One-off Basis

A Sharing button is enabled on the record detail page if OWD is set to Private or Public Read Only for any object. The record owner, or users that are higher in the role hierarchy, can share records with other users on a one-off basis. Currently, Lightning Experience doesn't support the manual-sharing feature. Therefore, if you want to use manual sharing, switch back to Salesforce Classic. Currently, the Lead object's OWD is set as Private.

Let's go back to another business scenario with Pamela Kline. At this point, she is well-versed in role hierarchy, OWD, and sharing settings, and she has successfully set up role hierarchies for GoC. Now, she wants to share records manually with user Brent Bassi by leveraging the manual-sharing feature. Brent Bassi currently has Read/Write access.

To fulfill the new requests, Pamela does the following using manual sharing.

1. She clicks the Sharing button, as shown in Figure 3-7, which directs her to a new window.

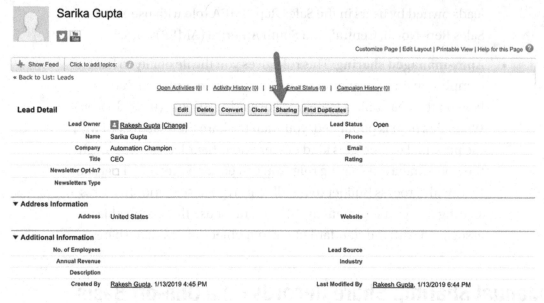

Figure 3-7. *Manual sharing*

2. She clicks the Add button.

3. She then selects one of the following options to share records with Brent (see Figure 3-8).

- Customer Portal Users

- Manager Subordinates Groups

- Manager Groups

- Partner Users

- Personal Groups

- Portal Roles

- Portal Roles and Subordinates

- Public Groups

- Roles

- Roles and Internal Subordinates

- Roles, Internal and Portal Subordinates

- Territories

- Territories and Subordinates

- Users

4. Finally, she clicks the Save button.

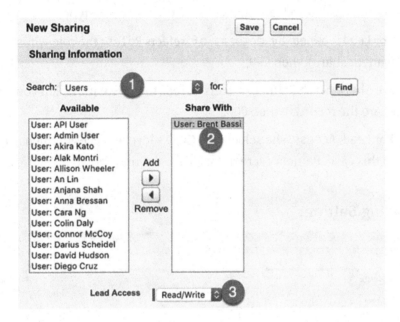

Figure 3-8. *Select an option to share records*

Owner-based Sharing: A Way to Share Records Automatically

Pamela is given a new task: share all records owned by the CFO with the COO and make sure the records between the CFO and the COO continue to be shared going forward. Currently, the Lead object OWD is set to Private.

Pamela performs the following steps to conquer this task using owner-based sharing.

1. She navigates to Setup (gear icon) ➤ Setup ➤ SETTINGS ➤ ➤ Security ➤ Sharing Settings.

2. She locates the Lead Sharing Rules list.

3. Pamela clicks the New button to create a new rule and is redirected to a new window where she must enter the label, rule name, and description. As a good practice, Pamela always writes a description so other administrators or developers can understand why she created this rule.

a. She selects "Based on record owner" for the rule type.

b. For Lead: owned by members of, selects Roles (the role whose records you want to share), then CFO.

c. For Share with, Pamela selects Roles (the role with which you want to share the records), then COO.

d. For Lead Access, she selects the COO's level of access, which is Read Only in this case. Pamela's screen looks like the one shown in Figure 3-9.

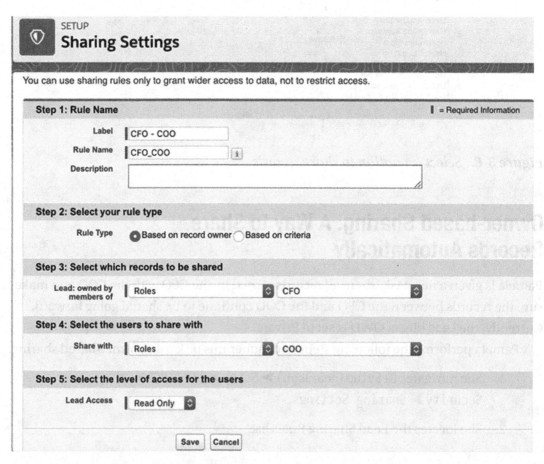

Figure 3-9. Defining owner-based sharing

4.   She clicks the Save button.

Salesforce recalculates the sharing settings. The requested changes are put into effect only after Salesforce is done recalculating the sharing settings.

Apex-Managed Sharing: A Way to Manage Complex Sharing in Seconds

When all other sharing rules can't fulfill your requirements, then you should use Apex to share records. Apex enables you to handle complex business scenarios. For example, let's say you have a field on the Lead object known as Potential Owner (User lookup). When this field is populated, you must share the Lead record with the potential owner. This kind of scenario is handled easily through Apex-managed sharing. You can write either Apex Trigger or Flow with Process Builder to handle this type of scenario. To access shared objects programmatically, you must specify the shared object whose records you want to share. Flow and Process Builder to create Apex-managed sharing are discussed in Chapter 7.

Deferring Sharing Calculations: Postpone Automatic Sharing Recalculation

Natively, every single change to the role hierarchy, groups, sharing rules, territory hierarchy, user roles, team membership, and ownership of records triggers sharing recalculations automatically. To suspend recalculation temporarily after making bulk changes, you must "raise a ticket" with Salesforce. By so doing, you can make the changes and then run sharing recalculations at a time when it is least disruptive to your users. Let's look at this concept more closely.

For instance, if you are modifying OWD for an object, such as from Public Read Only to Public Read/Write, your changes take effect only after Salesforce runs a recalculation process. Recalculation may take minutes or hours to complete, depending on your organization's data volume and customization. Similarly, if you modify a user's role, Salesforce runs all sharing rules again! For each update, Salesforce recalculates all access rights and sharing rules. As a result, if a user owns a lot of accounts and other records, the recalculation takes a long time to complete. If the recalculation runs in the background, then you won't be able to create new sharing rules or modify any security settings (such as OWD or the sharing rule) for that specific object in Salesforce (see Figure 3-10).

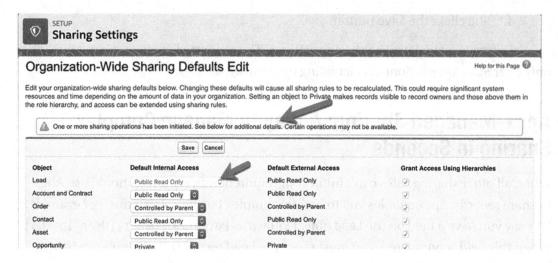

Figure 3-10. *Sharing recalculation message*

To avoid this snag, you must enable the Defer Sharing Calculations feature by raising a support ticket with Salesforce (see Figure 3-11). If you have an object that uses sharing and happens to have a large volume of records, and you need to make bulk changes (such as a periodical realignment requiring a hierarchy change) on that object, then deferring automatic sharing calculations is your best bet. When Defer Sharing Calculations is enabled by support, you can suspend the automatic sharing recalculation temporarily and run it when it is least disruptive to your users.

Defer Sharing Calculations
Help for this Page

You may want to suspend sharing calculations if you're making changes that affect a lot of records, roles, territories, groups, users, or sharing rules. On this page you can suspend automatic group membership and sharing rule calculations, which you can resume later at your discretion.

Group Membership Calculations
Group Membership Calculations Help

We calculate group membership any time you make changes to roles, territories, groups, users, or you change ownership of portal accounts.

[Suspend] [Resume]

Group membership calculations are enabled.

Suspending group membership calculations also suspends sharing rule calculations. Resuming group membership calculations requires a full recalculation of sharing rules, which may take a long time depending on the size of your organization.

Sharing Rule Calculations
Sharing Rule Calculations Help

We calculate sharing rules any time you create, edit or delete sharing rules, or make changes to roles, territories, or public groups participating in sharing rules.

[Suspend] [Resume] [Recalculate]

Sharing rule calculations are enabled.

Once suspended, resuming sharing rule calculations requires a full recalculation, which may take a long time depending on the size of your organization.

Figure 3-11. *Defer sharing calculations to postpone automatic sharing recalculation*

To summarize, OWD, role hierarchies, and sharing rules are tools that enable record sharing with users. Profiles and permission sets are used to control users' ability to perform actions on these records, such as the ability to delete records owned by users who do not have delete permission through either profiles or permission sets. In some cases, profiles and permission sets bypass OWD, role hierarchies, and sharing rules.

Profiles: A Way to Control Actions Users Can Take on a Record

Profiles are a way to customize the overall Salesforce experience. They are used to define data security by granting object and field-level permissions that decide the set of fields users can access and the ability to perform actions on records. Profiles have certain permissions that can be used to grant, restrict, or bypass user access. Role hierarchies with OWD and sharing rules decide record-level access. Profiles determine which records (in terms of fields) users can see and actions they can perform.

Types of Profiles

There are two types of profiles in Salesforce.

- **Standard** is an out-of-the-box profile built into any Salesforce org. Standard profiles cannot be deleted.

- **Custom** is created by cloning a standard profile.

The major difference between standard and custom profiles is that some parts of the standard profile can't be edited. For example, a standard profile's system, app, and object permissions can't be changed. Unlike custom profiles, which can be deleted if users are not assigned to them, standard profiles cannot be deleted.

Profiles contain system and object-specific permissions that override OWD.

- **View All Data**: This is a *system permission* that can be used to override OWD. For example, if you grant View All Data permission to users with the Marketing Executive role, then they can *view all records from all objects* regardless of their role or OWD.

- **Modify All Data**: This is a *system permission* that can be used to override OWD. For example, if you grant Modify All Data permission to users with the Marketing Executive role, then they can *modify all records from all objects* regardless of their role or OWD.

- **View All**: This is an *object-specific permission* that can be granted manually for each object. For example, if you grant View All permission to users with the Innovation Associate role for the Lead object, then they can *view all records of the* Lead *object* regardless of their role or OWD.

- **Modify All**: This is an *object-specific permission* that can be granted manually for each object. For example, if you grant Modify All permission to users with the Innovation Associate role, then they can *modify all records of the* Lead *object* regardless of their role or OWD.

As a rule of thumb, always create a custom profile by cloning it from a standard Read Only profile. The reason behind this is that the Read Only profile comes with minimal permission that can be modified easily.

Permission Sets

In Salesforce, users can have one—*and only one*—profile assigned to them. For example, Michelle White works as the COO at GoC. In the coming week, CFO Shannon Zadnowicz plans to go on vacation for two weeks. As a result, Michelle must cover Shannon by performing the duties of COO and CFO. Therefore, Michelle needs more access to Salesforce to perform both duties concomitantly. Because it is not possible to assign two profiles to a user, you must grant Michelle more access via permission sets.

Permission sets allow a system administrator to grant a group of settings and permissions to users beyond the users' existing profile. Via permission sets, the administrator can grant users access to various apps and functions their profile currently does not include. The settings available in permission sets are similar to profiles, but they extend users' functional access without changing their profiles.

Settings That Can Be Granted Through Permission Sets

The following is a list of major settings that can be granted to users via permission sets.

- **Assigned apps** grant access to assigned apps.

- **Object settings** grant the following permissions on an object.

  - Tab settings

  - Record-type settings

  - Object permissions

  - Field-level permissions

- **App permissions** grant *specific permissions* to users within an app.

- **Apex class and Visualforce page access** grant Apex classes and Visualforce page access to users.

- **Service providers** grant access to a service provider when single sign-on is enabled.

- **Custom permission** grants permission to access custom processes and apps.

- **System permissions** define permissions that apply across apps, such as View Encrypted Field, Modify All Data, and so on.

At runtime, user access is determined by the combined permissions granted via profiles *and* permission sets.

Granting Object Access

Using profiles and permission sets, a system administrator controls actions users can perform on a record.

Let's revisit Pamela Kline in another scenario. Currently, users with the Sales Rep-APAC role do not have permission to delete the records they own. As a result, Pamela needs to grant delete access to the following users (3 of 20) from the Sales Rep-APAC profile.

- Rakesh Gupta

- Sarika Gupta

- Munira Majmundar

To manage this task, Pamela uses permission sets instead of creating a new profile for the three Sales Rep-APAC users. In the future, the same permission set can be used for other users from any other or the same profile.

Pamela performs the following steps to meet this new requirement.

1. Pamela clicks Setup (gear icon) ➤ Setup ➤ ADMINISTRATION ➤ Users ➤ Permission Sets and then clicks the New button.

2. She is redirected to a new screen where she enters the label, API name, and description. She also selects User License from the drop-down menu and leaves it blank.

3. Pamela clicks the Save button.

4. Under the Apps section, Pamela clicks Object Settings and selects the Leads object.

5. Pamela clicks Edit and navigates to Object Permissions.

6. She selects Delete, as shown in Figure 3-12. When she does this, the system selects the Read and Edit permissions automatically.

Object Permissions

Permission Name	Enabled
Read	☑
Create	☐
Edit	☑
Delete	☑
View All	☐
Modify All	☐

Figure 3-12. *Permissions that control use access for an object*

7. Pamela clicks the Save button.

8. She assigns the permission set to the users stipulated in the business requirement.

Note   To learn more about assigning a permission set to users, see the Trailhead module at `https://trailhead.salesforce.com/en/content/learn/modules/wave_enable_setup/wave_set_up_permissions`.

If you plan to assign a permission set to all users who have the same user license type, the best practice is to associate that user license with the permission set. But, if you plan to assign a permission set to users with different user licenses (or users who might have different licenses in the future), it is probably best to create a permission set without a user license type.

Managing Field-level Security

So far, we've examined record-level accessibility, identifying which records are accessible by users, including OWD, role hierarchies, and sharing rules. Now, let's switch to studying field visibility.

Data is the new gold. Therefore, the importance of safeguarding and nurturing your customers' or prospects' data is difficult to overstate, for this is the path to gaining customer and prospect trust, acquisition, and retention. Data security is critical to preventing data breaches. In every CRM, there are some key fields a business may want to hide from all users, such as a Social Security number, bank details, a tax ID, and so on. Salesforce allows system administrators to use field-level security to hide fields or make them Read Only for specific profiles. There are four different ways to set field-level security.

1. Through a profile

2. Through a permission set

3. From an object field

4. Via field accessibility

Through a Profile

Remember, at runtime, user access is determined by the combined permissions granted via profiles *and* permission sets. Let's examine how to set field-level security at the profile level by giving Pamela Kline a new task. She must hide the Birthdate field on the Contact object from users assigned to the Standard User profile.

To handle these requests, Pamela performs the following steps.

1. She clicks Setup (gear icon) ➤ Setup ➤ ADMINISTRATION ➤ Users ➤ Profiles and then System User profile.

2. Under the Apps section, Pamela clicks Object Settings and then selects the Contact object.

3. Pamela clicks Edit and navigates to the Field Permission section.

4. She removes Read(1) access and Edit(2) access from the Birthdate field, as shown in Figure 3-13.

Field Permissions

Field Name	Read Access	Edit Access
Account Name	☑	☑
Assistant	☑	☑
Asst. Phone	☑	☑
Birthdate	☐	☐
Contact Currency	☑	☑
Contact Owner	☑	☑
Contact Record Type	☑	☑
Created By	☑	☐
Data.com Key	☑	☑
Department	☑	☑
Description	☑	☑
Do Not Call	☐	☐
Email	☑	☑
Email Opt Out	☐	☐
Fax	☑	☑
Fax Opt Out	☐	☐
Home Phone	☑	☑
Last Modified By	☑	☐
Last Stay-in-Touch Request Date	☑	☐
Last Stay-in-Touch Save Date	☑	☐

Figure 3-13. *Field permissions are used to control field read/edit access*

5. She clicks the Save button.

Points to Remember

- If you are changing the default access, such as from Public Read Only to Public Read/Write, your changes take effect *after Salesforce completes running the recalculation process.*

- Users with Edit permission on the price books—granted via profiles or permission sets—get access to all price books, regardless of OWD.

- When you select the `Grant Access Using Hierarchies` field, it provides access to people who are above the owner in the role hierarchy.

- If your sharing model for related opportunities is Public Read Only, then a `Sharing` button may appear on an Account detail page even though your sharing model for Account is Public Read/Write.

- It is not possible to include high-volume portal users in sharing rules because they don't have roles and can't be included in a public group.

- The sharing rule is always used to open access. If you want to restrict record access, you must modify your organization's OWD.

- Salesforce doesn't allow anyone to delete the `Standard User` profile.

- If you select the `Read Only` check box under object field-level security, then the `Visible` check box is selected automatically.

- Make sure to enable field history tracking for a field if you want to track which users are changing field values and when they are doing so.

- When working with object and field access, *the most restrictive setting wins*.

- When working with record access, *the most permissive setting wins*.

- To increase the limit on a sharing rule, raise a case with Salesforce support. By default, you can define up to 300 user sharing rules, including up to 50 criteria-based sharing rules.

- The external access level for an object can't be more permissive than the internal access level.

Hands-on Exercises

The following exercises give you more practice with the platform, which ultimately will help you gain mastery of it and assist you in preparing for the certification examination. Remember, these are hands-on exercises, and you can find the answers at the back of the book in the appendix, but try to implement them in your Salesforce org, which is the primary goal of doing them.

1. Create a custom object known as Address (Address__c). Then, check OWD for this object under Security Setting. Test your knowledge by selecting one of the following options.

   a. Private

   b. Public Read/Write

   c. Public Full Access

   d. Public Read Only

2. Set OWD for Address (Address__c) in such a way that if users don't own a record in the Address object, then they can't access the record.

3. Dennis Williams, a system administrator at GoC, must meet the following requirements for Address (Address__c).

   a. All users can't access address records.

      i. CEO: Can access all records

      ii. COO: Can access all records

      iii. Sales Rep-EMEA: Users in this role can access all records.

      iv. Sales Rep-APAC: Two of the 20 users in this role can access all records. The remaining cannot access a single record.

      v. Sales Rep-AMER: Users in this role can access all records.

   b. Pamela Kline, the system administrator, owns all records.

   c. Users can only view, but cannot edit or delete, any record in the Address__c object.

4. Dennis Williams is tasked to create a field to store Social Security numbers. He wants to make sure that only a system administrator and key users, including the following, can access the Social Security Number field.

    a. Rakesh Gupta

    b. Sarika Gupta

    c. Munira Majmundar

5. Dennis must share ten records, which are currently owned by VP Sales, with a user belonging to the Dir. Product role. What kind of sharing mechanism would you suggest to him? Select one of the following options.

    a. OWD

    b. Owner-based sharing

    c. Manual sharing

    d. Criteria-based sharing

    e. Permission set

6. Dennis is having a hard time debugging one record-sharing problem. Please help him solve it. Here is the complete scenario.

    a. Object: Address__c

    b. OWD: Public Read/Write

    c. Grant Access Using Hierarchies: True

    d. Owned by system administrator

    e. The company CEO (Rakesh Gupta) is not able to delete this record. Why?

7. Dennis is gradually grasping the concept of the sharing architecture. However, he is having a hard time debugging one record-sharing problem. Please help him solve it. Here is the complete scenario.

    a. Object: `Address__c`

    b. OWD: Public Read Only

    c. `Grant Access Using Hierarchies`: True

    d. Owned by system administrator

    e. The company CEO (Rakesh Gupta) is not able to edit the record. Why?

8. Dennis wants to implement opportunity management at GoC, but he is a bit confused with one of the requirements. Because you now have a better understanding of record sharing, please help him select the appropriate sharing architecture to fulfill the following needs.

    a. When the opportunity amount is greater than US$1,000,000, share the record with VP Product.

    b. However, autorevoke record access from VP Product if the opportunity amount drops to less than US$1,000,000.

9. Help Dennis select the appropriate object-level security for the Lead object where 3 of 20 Sales Rep-AMER users can create new Lead records, but the remaining 17 users can only view the Lead records. List all the Salesforce features that Dennis can use to solve this requirement.

10. Dennis has a new request to tackle: all users from the Eng. Team role must be able to modify all records from the `Lead` object. What is your suggestion for Dennis to solve this?

11. Dennis is tasked to share leads that have an annual revenue of more than US$10,000,000 and belong to the London office. The owner is Shannon Zadnowicz, CFO at GoC. What is your recommendation for Dennis to solve this?

12. Currently, all users can see all Lead records. Dennis is tasked to make the following modifications.

    a. Except for users Rakesh Gupta and Munira Majmundar, all users can see all Lead records.

    b. Rakesh Gupta and Munira Majmundar are not allowed to access any records.

    How can Dennis meet these requirements?

13. Dennis is implementing account management at GoC and has a new task: only users with access to an Account record can access related Contact records. Help Dennis fulfill this requirement.

14. Dennis needs to share the Lead record with Dir. Product, just for 48 hours, if the annual revenue is greater than US$100,000,000. Help Dennis handle this task.

Summary

This chapter covered OWD and how it affects record accessibility, followed by an in-depth look at role hierarchies. It also studied various sharing rules available in Salesforce and reviewed the functionality of profiles and permission sets. Finally, it looked at object and field-level security and their use cases.

Chapter 4 takes a deep dive into Lightning Experience customization.

CHAPTER 4

Customizing the User Interface

Abstract

Chapter 3 studied the Salesforce sharing architecture, including OWD and role hierarchies. It discussed how different real-world problems can be solved by using various sharing mechanisms and looked at how profiles and permission sets play a key role in handling object- and field-level security in Salesforce.

This chapter covers the Lightning Experience, creating dynamic Lightning pages, and enabling custom buttons, links, and actions.

A Deep Dive into Lightning Experience

Unlike Salesforce Classic, the engine behind Lightning Experience is a user's device agnostic. What does that mean? Well, mobile use has been increasing exponentially—be it at the workplace or for personal use. Sales reps are now using mobile devices to find potential customers, use social media to connect with customers, and more. Lightning Experience mimics the way sales reps work on a mobile platform and thus provides a seamless experience across platforms.

Lightning Experience is a fresh and productive user interface. It is aimed at helping sales reps close more deals quickly by providing flexible, intuitive, and interactive tools. The tools enable the reps to focus on deals, customers, and activities that promise the greatest returns. The sophisticated Lightning Experience user interface, coupled

R. Gupta, *Salesforce Platform App Builder Certification Companion*, Certification Study Companion Series

with Einstein's predictive modeling, turbocharges sales rep productivity exponentially by enabling them to take the step at the right time, with the right customer, on the right deal.

In addition to being faster, Lightning Experience enables system administrators to deliver a pleasant user experience by quickly building a Lighting page to suit a user's working style or needs. Lightning Experience uses a component-based design pattern. This means that to build a Lightning page, all you have to do is place components on a page at the location of your choice! Let's go ahead and see what Lightning Experience looks like.

The Lightning Experience Navigation Menu

Similar to the navigation menu in Salesforce Classic, Lightning Experience also displays tabs across the top of the screen. Furthermore, with Lightning Experience, as with Classic, end users can customize the navigation menu to suit their working style and needs. Via the navigation menu, users can take the following actions (see Figure 4-1).

- Switch apps via App Launcher

- Identify the current app's name

- Access recent records

- Create new records

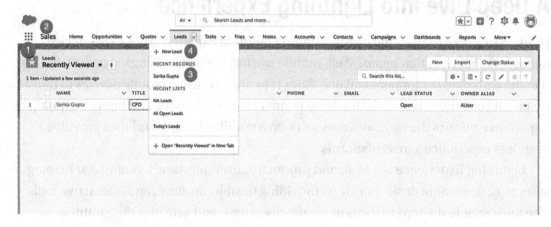

Figure 4-1. *Lightning app navigation menu*

In addition, end users can customize the navigation menu (including reordering and adding/removing tabs) by adding the following items to the menu.

- Standard objects

- Custom objects

- Home tab

- Visualforce tabs

- Lightning component tabs

- Web tabs

- Canvas apps via Visualforce tabs

The App Launcher in Lightning Experience

As mentioned, Lightning Experience allows a user to switch between apps using App Launcher. Apps show up as large tiles under All Apps. The apps list can include standard apps, custom apps, and connected apps, such as G Suite. Other items, such as custom objects, tasks, events, and feeds, show up under All Items. Users can find apps by searching for the app name in the search box (1 in Figure 4-2) or by using the App Launcher (2 in Figure 4-2).

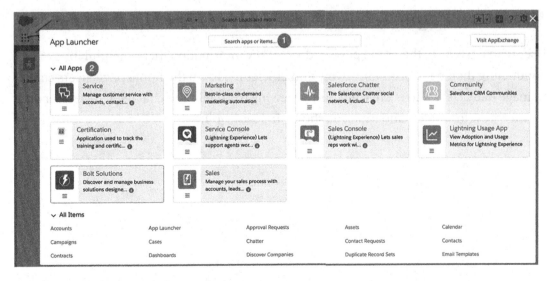

Figure 4-2. *Access App Launcher*

In addition, users can also personalize the order of the apps on this page by dragging the tiles per their needs (see Figure 4-3). However, be aware that a Salesforce administrator can override the app sort order set by users.

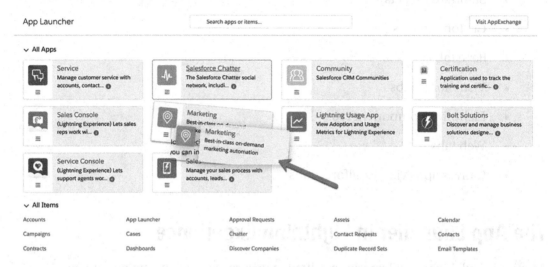

Figure 4-3. *Rearrange apps in Lightning*

The app menu lists all apps installed in the org. However, the apps users see in App Launcher and the app menu may vary based on visibility settings and user permissions set on their profile.

The Home Page

Users can customize the home page to display key information that is helpful in conducting their daily tasks effectively and efficiently. From the home page, users can manage daily tasks and events, including viewing top deals, the chat feed, recent records, quarterly performance, and more, as shown in Figure 4-4.

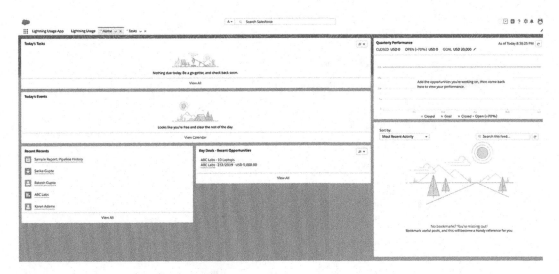

Figure 4-4. *Lightning home page*

Furthermore, unlike Classic, with Lightning Experience, users can remove the Home tab from a Lightning app. A Home tab is no longer mandatory!

Global Search

What happens if users have tons of records in Salesforce? How can they get what they need quickly? Well, global search is there to rescue these users!

Global search finds what users are looking for by breaking a search term into small parts. The global search box is available at the top of every page in Lightning Experience. When users click the global search box, they see a drop-down of all recent items, as shown in Figure 4-5.

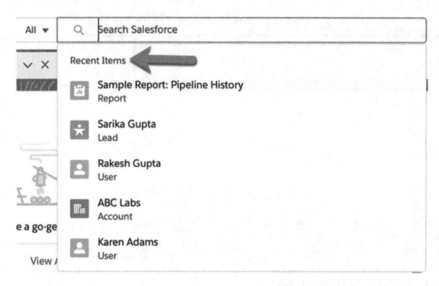

Figure 4-5. *Access global search*

If users start typing in the search box, the list updates dynamically with matches from all searchable objects. When users see what they are looking for, then they can select it quickly. As the example in Figure 4-6 shows, if a user types sari in the search box, the system shows all records that contain sari anywhere.

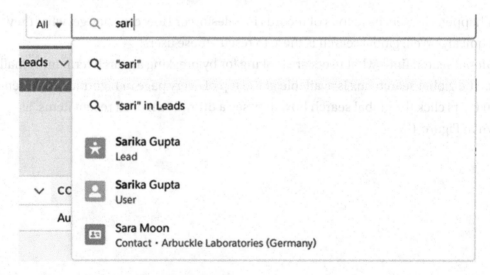

Figure 4-6. *Search on a partial word*

If users click the global search box from an object-specific view, like from a Leads page, then the global search looks for leads based on the search string.

Creating Dynamic Lightning Pages

The beauty of Salesforce's Lightning Experience is that it allows users to create dynamic pages without writing a single line of code. Such features deliver a high level of sophistication and customization in Lightning Experience that is missing from Classic.

Controlling Component Visibility

Let's return to Robin Guzman, a Salesforce administrator at GoC. His basic understanding of Lightning Experience—how to navigate within it and create a Lightning page—has increased greatly. He created a Lightning record page (Lead Record Page) for the Lead object and made it the org default (see Figure 4-7).

Figure 4-7. *Lead Lightning page*

Now, he wants to learn how to make the Files component dynamic on the Leads record page based on the logged-in user. Specifically, he wants to hide the Files component from the system administrator.

Robin does the following to solve the task by leveraging the component visibility setting.

1. He navigates to Setup (gear icon) ➤ Setup ➤ Object Manager ➤ Lead ➤ Lightning Record Pages and locates the Lead record page (see Figure 4-8).

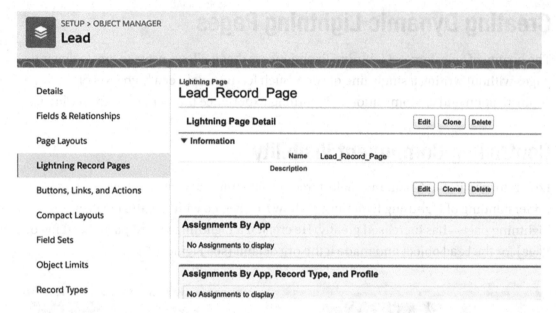

Figure 4-8. *Lightning record page*

2. He clicks Edit and navigates to Lightning App Builder.

3. To add component visibility, Robin clicks the Files component (1 in Figure 4-9) and then clicks the + Add Filter button (2 in Figure 4-9), which is available under Set Component Visibility.

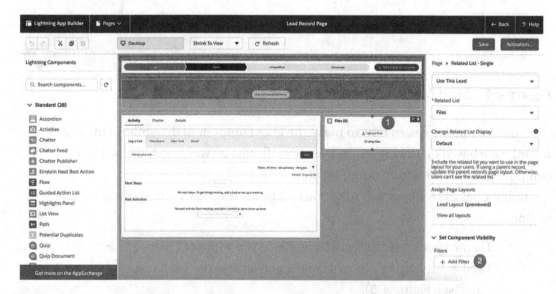

Figure 4-9. *Lightning App Builder*

4. This action redirects Robin to a new window, where he selects the
   filter type, field, operator, and value as follows.

   a. For Filter Type, she selects Advanced.

   b. For Field, he selects Profile Name by navigating to User ➤
      Profile ➤ Name.

   c. For Operator, he selects Not Equal.

   d. For Value, he selects System Administrator.

Robin's screen now looks like the one shown in Figure 4-10.

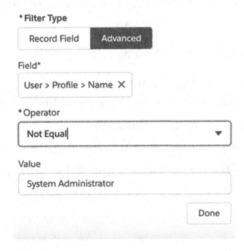

Figure 4-10. *Set component visibility*

5. He clicks the Done button.

6. After completing all configurations, Robin saves the Lightning
   page by clicking the Save button.

When Robin clicks the Save button, Salesforce recalculates the sharing settings of
the components added to the Lead Lightning record page and removes Files component
access from a system administrator. This may be an eye-opener! It is important to
know and understand that even a system administrator is not immune from not having
visibility access to a component. Powerful indeed!

Likewise, users can control the visibility of components on the Lightning record
page, app page, home page, and Lightning for Outlook page.

Lightning Page Assignment

In Lightning Experience, users can set Lightning page assignments based on different parameters. For example, users can create multiple Lead Lightning record pages and then assign them based on the following parameters.

- Assign a page as an org default.

- Assign a page as the default for specific Lightning apps. For instance, users can have multiple Lead Lightning pages based on different Lightning apps. Users can assign Lead record pages (Sales) to the Lightning Sales app. Similarly, they can assign Lead record pages (Service) to the Lightning Service app.

- Use a combination of app, record type, and profile.

Robin has now become a pro in creating Lightning record pages and knows how to show and hide components from them. He created a Lightning record page for Lead called Lead Record Page (Sales). Next, he wants to assign this record page to the Sales app so that whenever users open the Lightning Sales app, they see this page for the Lead record. To do this, Robin performs the following steps using the page visibility setting.

1. He navigates to Setup (gear icon) ➤ Setup ➤ Object Manager ➤ Lead ➤ Lightning Record Pages and then locates Lead Record Page (Sales).

2. He clicks Edit and navigates to Lightning App Builder.

3. To add component visibility, he clicks the Activation button in the top-right corner. The system redirects Robin to a new window to set up the Lightning page assignment.

4. Robin clicks the APP DEFAULT tab and then the Assign as App Default button to set the Lightning page for the Lighting Sales app, as shown in Figure 4-11.

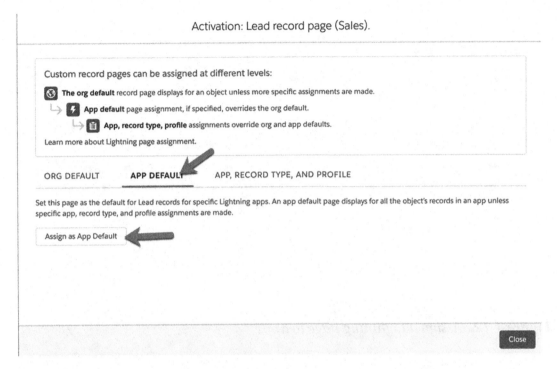

Figure 4-11. Set Lightning page assignment

5. Robin selects the app: Sales.

6. He clicks the Next button, as shown in Figure 4-12.

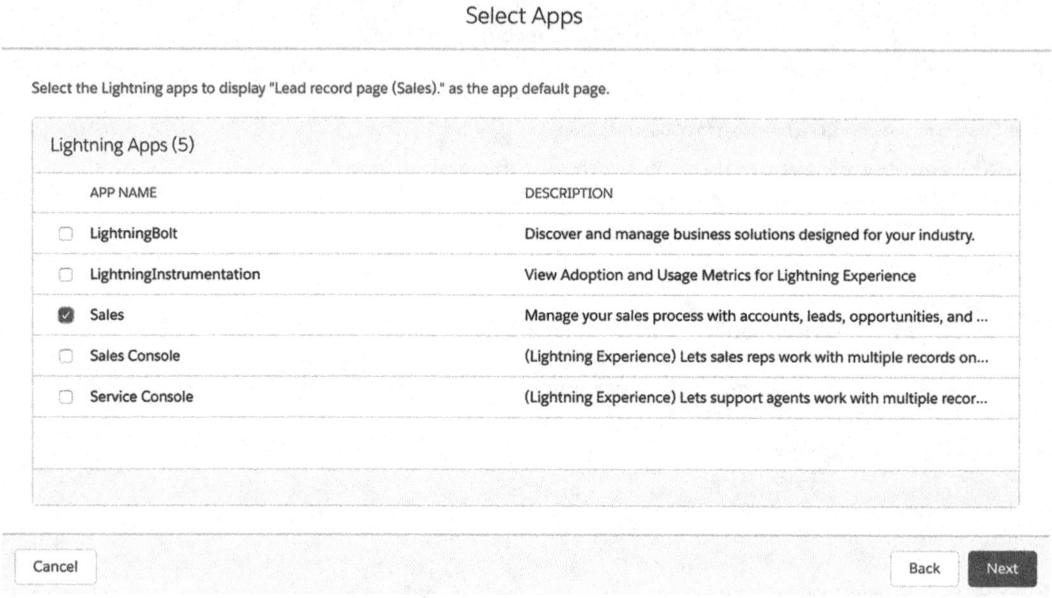

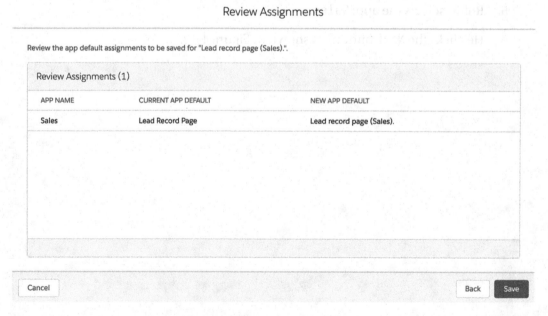

Figure 4-12. *Assign a Lightning page to apps*

7. He then reviews the assignment and clicks the Save button, as shown in Figure 4-13.

Figure 4-13. *Review the Lightning page assignment*

After Robin clicks the Save button, Salesforce recalculates the sharing settings and page assignment for the Lead object. Going forward, users will see the Lead Record Page (Sales) when they select the Lightning Sales app and open the Lead record.

Use Case for Custom Buttons and Links

Each business unit has its own set of requirements that may require specific configuration. For example, if users are responsible for managing vendors and they want to allow access to an Account page from outside the org (e.g., for a vendor management system), then Salesforce requires users to create a custom button or a link.

A custom button or a link allows users to integrate Salesforce data from external applications or data from a company's internal portal, for example. The ability to access Salesforce data from an external application—with a click of a button or a link—boosts user productivity several-fold.

In Lightning Experience, when custom buttons and links are added to a page layout, they appear in different regions of a Lightning page. The following are the different types of custom buttons and links users can create in Salesforce.

- **List button**: Appears in a related list of an object's record page.

- **Detail page link**: Appears in the Links section of the details page of an object's record.

- **Detail page button**: Appears in the action menu in the highlight panel of an object's record page.

Let's rejoin Robin, who has just received the task to create a custom button on a Lead page to search for a lead company using Google Search. After clicking the button, it should open a Google Search page to find details about the lead company.

Robin performs the following steps to create a custom button.

1. He navigates to Setup (gear icon) ➤ Setup ➤ Object Manager ➤ Lead ➤ Buttons, Links and Actions.

2. He clicks the New button or link, which redirects him to a new window to set up a custom button. Once there, he works his way through by entering information as follows.

   a. **Label**: Robin names a custom Open Google Search button.

   b. **Name**: This field autopopulates based on the label.

c. **Description**: Robin writes some meaningful text so that other developers and administrators can easily understand why the custom button was created in the first place.

d. **Display Type**: He selects the Detail Page button.

e. **Behavior**: He selects Display in the existing window without a sidebar.

f. **Content Source**: He selects the URL, then pastes the following into the large text box: https://www.google.com/search?q={!Lead.Company}.

Robin's screen looks like the one depicted in Figure 4-14.

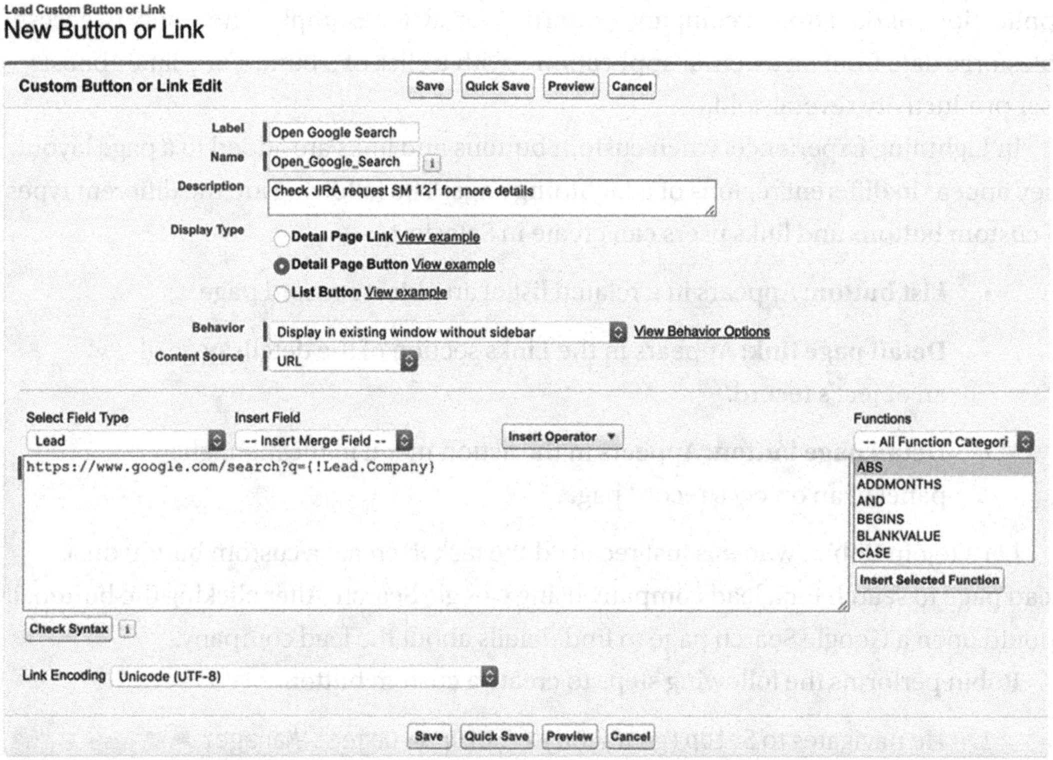

Figure 4-14. *Creating a custom button*

3. Robin clicks the Save button.

4. Next, he adds a new custom button to the Lead page layout by navigating to Setup (gear icon) ➤ Setup ➤ Object Manager ➤ Lead ➤ Page layouts.

5. Then, he clicks the Edit link and drags and drops the custom Open Google Search button to the Salesforce Mobile and Lightning Experience Actions section of the page layout, as shown in Figure 4-15.

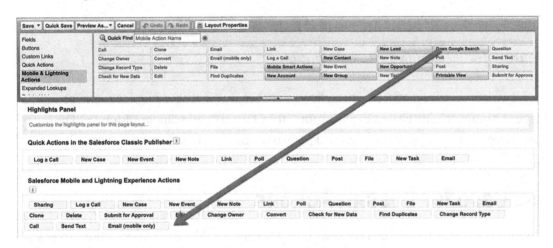

Figure 4-15. *Adding a button to Lightning Experience*

6. Robin clicks the Save button.

7. He makes sure to whitelist the https://www.goggle.com URL.

Going forward, the Open Google Search custom button is available in the Lead record page's highlight panel, as shown in Figure 4-16.

Figure 4-16. *Accessing the custom button*

Likewise, users can add a custom link to an Account's record page to make an account manager's life easier. Furthermore, they can also add Sales guideline PDF custom links to the Opportunity record page to improve a team's productivity.

Use Case for Custom Actions

Actions allow users to perform certain activities very quickly, such as creating records, updating records, sending emails, logging calls, calling a Lightning component, executing Lightning Flow, and calling a Visualforce page. With custom actions, users save precious time by getting quick access to important information. There are two types of actions available to users: object-specific and global.

- **Object-specific actions**: Object-specific actions have automatic relationships to other records. The actions let users quickly create or update records, send emails, log calls, call Lightning components, execute Lightning Flow, and call a Visualforce page in the context of a particular object. A few examples of object-specific actions include the following.

  - Creating a custom action on `Opportunity` object to update `Stage` to `Closed Lost`, as shown in Figure 4-17.

Figure 4-17. *Updating the Opportunity object*

- Creating a Record Create action (Create Order) from Opportunity without leaving the Opportunity record page.

- **Global actions**: Users can create global actions in Setup and then put global actions anywhere on an object that supports actions. Using global actions, users can log calls, create records, send emails, call a Visualforce page, execute a Lightning component, and call Custom Canvas, all without leaving the page.

Chapter 6 discusses how to use custom actions to call Lightning Flow.

Points to Remember

- Users can't personalize the navigation bar when it contains more than 50 items.

- When a system administrator removes an item from an app, that item remains in users' personalized navigation bars. Then, if they so choose, users can delete the item.

- Lightning apps aren't available in Classic.

- The object-specific Send Email action is only available in cases.

- To show custom buttons, links, or actions in Lightning Experience, you must customize the Action section of a page layout. If you do not, then you see whichever default buttons, actions, and links are defined by Salesforce.

Hands-on Exercises

The following exercises give you more practice with the platform, which ultimately will help you gain mastery of it and assist you in preparing for the certification examination. Remember, these are hands-on exercises, and you can find the answers at the back of the book in the appendix, but try to implement them in your Salesforce org, which is the primary goal of doing them.

1. Edit a Lightning record page of a Lead object and explore different components. Test out its role and functionality.

2. Create a custom button to open a Yahoo News page for Account.

3. Dennis Williams, a system administrator at GoC, has received the following task: On an Account Lightning record page, hide the News component from those users that do not have Access Activities permission.

   How would you instruct Dennis to perform this task?

4. Dennis needs to create a quick action on the Lead object to update Status quickly to Unqualified, then add the quick action to all Lead record pages. How would you instruct Dennis to perform these tasks?

5. Create a custom Lightning app (named Sales Critical) and add the following tabs to it.

   - Home
   - Lead
   - Account

- Contact

- Opportunity

- Campaign

Then, list all your new findings, including app logo size, navigation style, and app personalization settings, and add a Utility Item section.

Summary

This chapter looked at an overview of Lightning Experience, followed by an in-depth study of the dynamic record pages. It also examined custom buttons, links, and action use cases with real-life examples. Chapter 5 examines how to improve and enrich data quality in Salesforce.

CHAPTER 5

Improving and Enriching Data Quality

Abstract

Chapter 4 looked at an overview of Lightning Experience and studied the dynamic record page. It discussed use cases for custom buttons, links, and actions using real-life examples.

This chapter overviews record types and looks at lookup filters and dependent lookups. More specifically, it examines formula fields, discusses a use case of a roll-up summary field, and examines the best way to write enterprise-level validation rules using custom permissions.

Record Types: A Better Way to Handle Varied Business Processes

Record types play a key role in Salesforce implementation. Without having a good understanding of them, developers or architects may end up devising an incorrect solution or writing code, which may turn out to be a suboptimal solution.

For example, suppose there is a custom object `Registrant` that is being used to store event participants. Depending on the value in the `Industry` field, a marketing director wants to display different fields on a page layout, as shown in Table 5-1. If the value in the `Industry` field is Manufacturing, then the director wants to display additional fields on a page layout, such as `Annual Income`, `Date of Birth`, or `Shift Hours`. If, however, the value in the `Industry` field is anything other than Manufacturing, the director does not want to display the additional fields.

113

R. Gupta, Salesforce Platform App Builder Certification Companion, Certification Study Companion Series

Table 5-1. *Representation the Data Marketing Director Wants to Capture*

Manufacturing	Other
First Name	First Name
Last NameE-mailEventIndustry (Manufacturing, Shipping, Consulting, and Other)	Last NameE-mailEventIndustry (Manufacturing, Shipping, Consulting, and Other)
PhoneAnnual Income*Date of Birth*	Phone
Shift Hours*	

There are various ways to meet this requirement. For example, you can write *validation rules* that state that whenever the value in the Industry field is Manufacturing, make the three other fields required. This requires users to populate the fields before they can save the record.

Even if the validation rule works, it will create a negative user experience because the required fields, because of the Manufacturing value in the Industry field, would not have a red asterisk attached to it.

Figure 5-1 demonstrates how developers can make fields required based on the value in the Industry field. This approach has the following issues.

1. First, it creates a negative user experience because the required fields (only when the value in the Industry field is Manufacturing) would not display a red asterisk next to it!

2. What happens if users select a value other than Manufacturing in the Industry field? In such a scenario, they would be able to *skip entering the data in the required fields because the validation rule would not trigger* if the value in the Industry field is anything other than Manufacturing. This situation creates a big dent in achieving and maintaining data integrity—to say the least!

    To avoid a negative user experience or avoid compromising data integrity, developers and architects must write a complex validation rule.

3. The validation rule route displays unnecessary fields on a page layout when a value other than Manufacturing is in the Industry field. In such a scenario, fields like Annual Income, Date of Birth, or Shift Hours would gobble up page layout real estate without adding any value—not to mention delivering a suboptimal user experience.

4. With the validation rules route, confusion, a negative user experience, and clutter in the page layout skyrockets if developers or architects are tasked with adding a few custom buttons or links to the page layout specific to the manufacturing industry!

Edit Adam Smith

Information

* Registrant Name	Adam Smith	Owner	Rakesh Gupta
First Name	Adam	Event	⭐ Virtual Dreamin ×
Last Name	Smith	Industry	Manufacturing ▼
Email	asmith@achamp.co	Phone	9876543219

Manufacturing Registrant Information

Date of Birth	📅	Annual Income	
	Please enter Date of Birth, as Registrant belongs to manufacturing industry.		Please enter Annual Income, as Registrant belongs to manufacturing industry.
Shift Hours	--None-- ▼		
	Please select shift hors, as Registrant belongs to manufacturing industry.		

Cancel   Save & New   Save

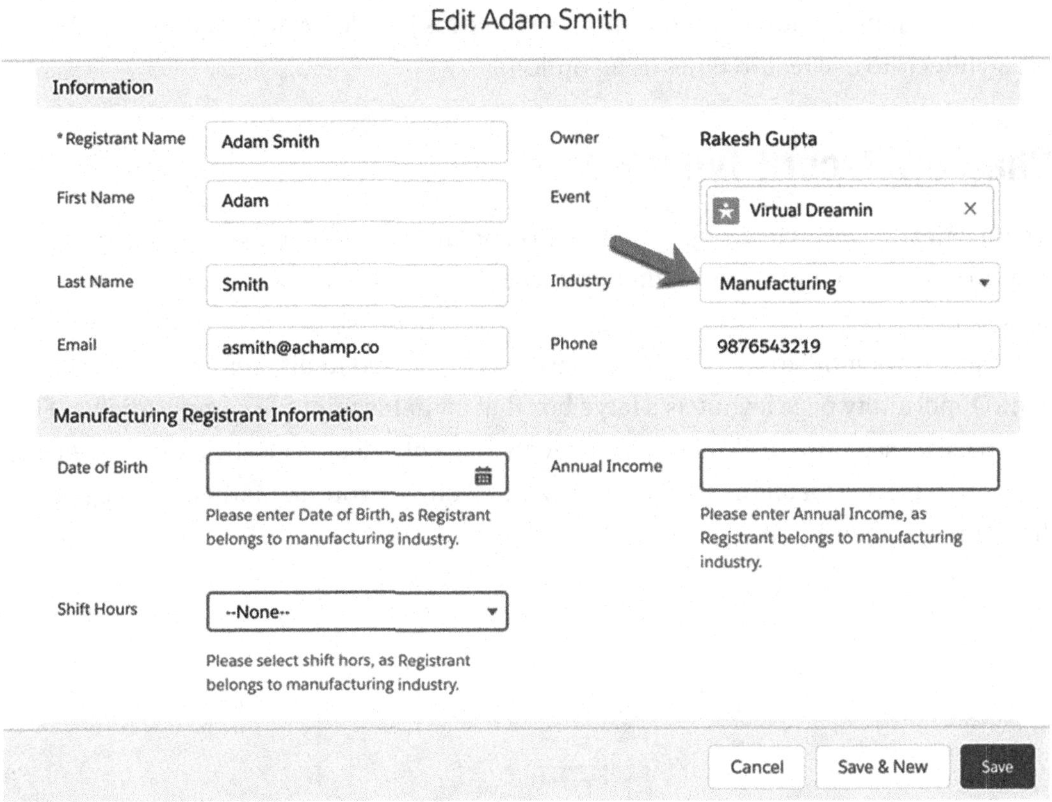

Figure 5-1. *Required fields based on the Industry drop-down*

Still not convinced the validation rules route may be a suboptimal solution? Well, let's take a look at another example.

Assume the marketing director is happy with the validation rules solution you provided and that it works as of today. However, the director now walks into your office and tasks you with a new requirement. She wants the value in the Industry field to be Shipping. When the value in the Industry field is Shipping, you need to create more than 40 fields. The marketing director also wants to gather additional data, such as participants' current job duties and bonuses, when the value is Shipping. To avoid confusion, a negative user experience, and clutter in the page layout, the director does not want the 40 fields to be displayed if the value in the Industry field is not Shipping.

In light of this situation, do you still think the validation rules route is an optimal solution? I don't think so, either. To conclude, because page layout doesn't allow users to show/hide fields based on the value of another field, the validation rules route falls short. Developing a solution for the various scenarios just described requires developers and architects to use record types as an option.

What Are Record Types?

Record types allow you to group similar fields and display them to users as necessary. They do so by enabling you to segment a particular object's fields/sections for specific uses.

Figure 5-2 demonstrates how a page layout is organized in different sections. Think of the Opportunity page layout as a large box that contains multiple compartments. The same page is displayed to all sales reps at every stage of a deal, regardless of whether the sales reps have use for all the fields on the page layout. As you saw earlier, this negatively affects productivity and the sales reps' experience.

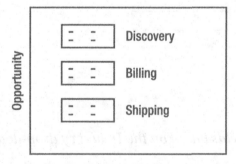

Figure 5-2. *A page layout is organized into different sections*

Record types to rescue! Record types help improve the sales rep experience by displaying appropriate sections/fields on a page layout based on an Opportunity stage. Record types are used mainly for two purposes.

- To show different page layouts based on conditions. For example, if an Opportunity stage is Closed Won or Closed Lost, then display the Read Only page layout.

- To show/hide picklist values. For example, if an Opportunity type is Existing business, then remove the following values from the Lead Source field.

  - Partner

  - Employee Referral

  - Other

As a developer, you can create three different page layouts—Discovery, Billing, and Shipping—and then display different fields on the page layout based on the value in the Opportunity stage field.

Table 5-2 represents the page layouts and their dependency based on the Opportunity stage. To control fields in page layouts based on the Opportunity stage, you need to use a record type.

Table 5-2. *Page Layouts and Their Dependency on the* Opportunity *Stage*

Page Layout	Stage
Discovery	Prospecting
Billing	Proposal/Price Quote
Shipping	Closed Won

Figure 5-3 demonstrates how record types control page layouts based on different stages. One record type can assign different page layouts to different profiles, or one record type can assign a single page layout to multiple profiles. In Figure 5-3, record type controls discovery page layouts 1 and 2 based on the profiles. So far, so good. Let's take this discussion one level up.

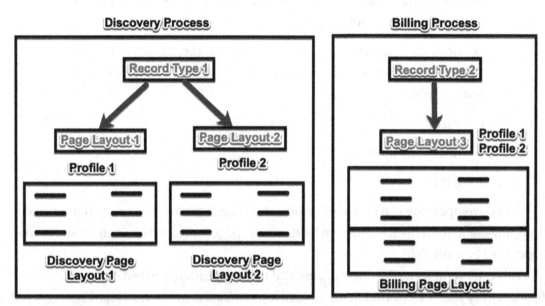

Figure 5-3. *Record types control page layouts*

Let's get back to our business scenario with Robin Guzman. He's received a request from his manager to configure the Registrant custom object based on Table 5-1.

To meet this request, Robin performs the following steps using record types and page layouts.

1. Robin navigates to Setup (gear icon) ➤ Setup ➤ Object Manager ➤ Create ➤ Custom Object and creates a new custom object, Registrant, and all the fields mentioned in Table 5-1.

2. Next, he creates two-page layouts by navigating to Setup (gear icon) ➤ Setup ➤ Object Manager ➤ Registrant ➤ Page Layouts.

    The Registrant page layout looks like Figure 5-4.

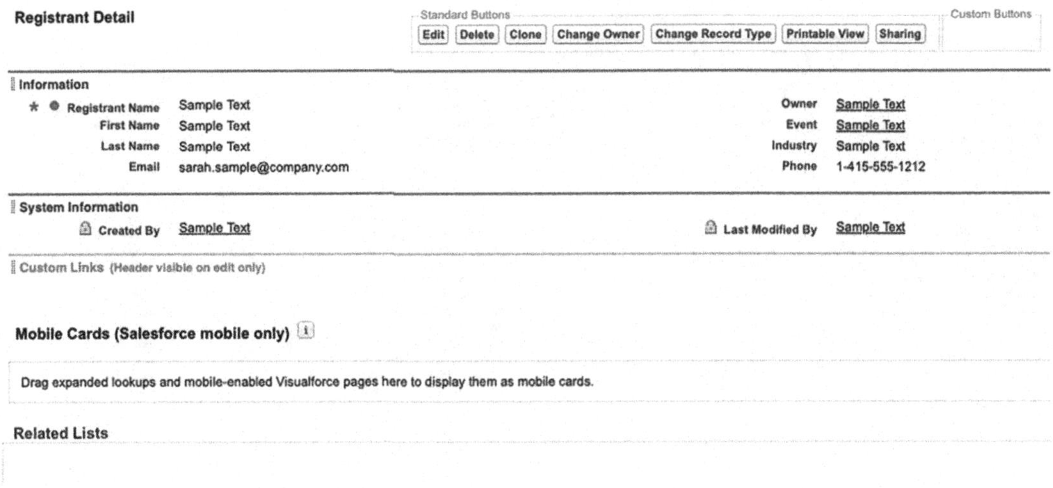

Figure 5-4. *Registrant page layout*

The Manufacturing Registrant page layout looks like Figure 5-5.

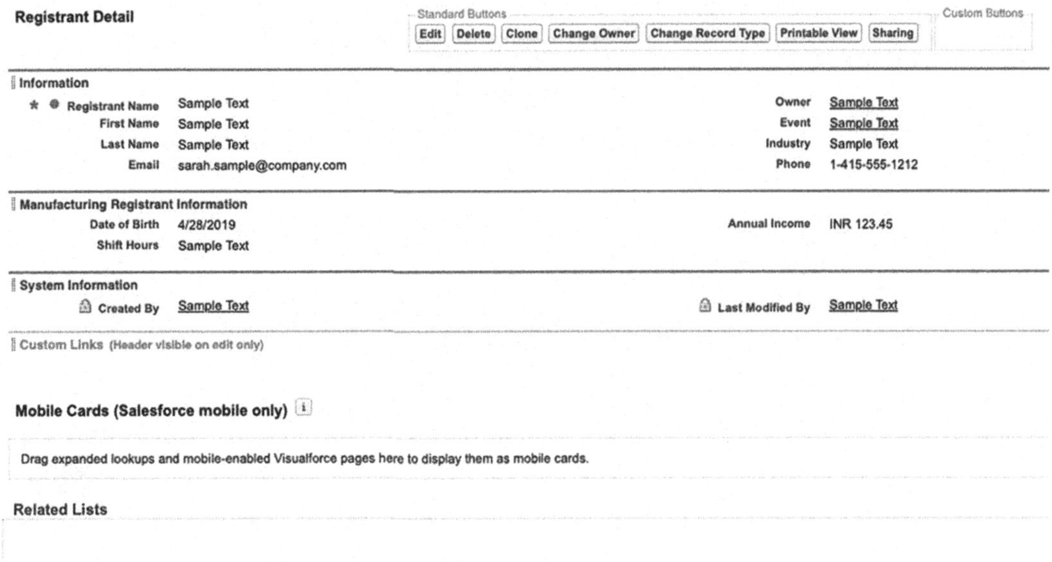

Figure 5-5. *Registrant page layout for manufacturing*

3. Robin creates two record types—Manufacturing and Others—and
    then assigns page layouts, as shown in Figure 5-6.

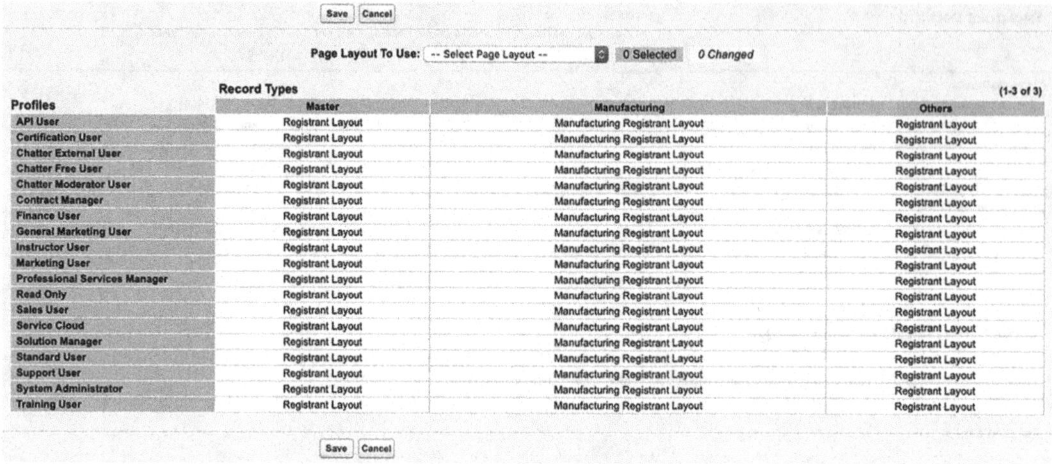

| | Save | Cancel | |

Page Layout To Use: -- Select Page Layout --   0 Selected   0 Changed

Profiles	Record Types		(1-3 of 3)
	Master	Manufacturing	Others
API User	Registrant Layout	Manufacturing Registrant Layout	Registrant Layout
Certification User	Registrant Layout	Manufacturing Registrant Layout	Registrant Layout
Chatter External User	Registrant Layout	Manufacturing Registrant Layout	Registrant Layout
Chatter Free User	Registrant Layout	Manufacturing Registrant Layout	Registrant Layout
Chatter Moderator User	Registrant Layout	Manufacturing Registrant Layout	Registrant Layout
Contract Manager	Registrant Layout	Manufacturing Registrant Layout	Registrant Layout
Finance User	Registrant Layout	Manufacturing Registrant Layout	Registrant Layout
General Marketing User	Registrant Layout	Manufacturing Registrant Layout	Registrant Layout
Instructor User	Registrant Layout	Manufacturing Registrant Layout	Registrant Layout
Marketing User	Registrant Layout	Manufacturing Registrant Layout	Registrant Layout
Professional Services Manager	Registrant Layout	Manufacturing Registrant Layout	Registrant Layout
Read Only	Registrant Layout	Manufacturing Registrant Layout	Registrant Layout
Sales User	Registrant Layout	Manufacturing Registrant Layout	Registrant Layout
Service Cloud	Registrant Layout	Manufacturing Registrant Layout	Registrant Layout
Solution Manager	Registrant Layout	Manufacturing Registrant Layout	Registrant Layout
Standard User	Registrant Layout	Manufacturing Registrant Layout	Registrant Layout
Support User	Registrant Layout	Manufacturing Registrant Layout	Registrant Layout
System Administrator	Registrant Layout	Manufacturing Registrant Layout	Registrant Layout
Training User	Registrant Layout	Manufacturing Registrant Layout	Registrant Layout

| | Save | Cancel | |

Figure 5-6. *Assigning page layouts based on record types and profiles*

Going forward, users have the option to select the record type before creating a Registrant record, as shown in Figure 5-7. Based on the record type, it displays the page layout.

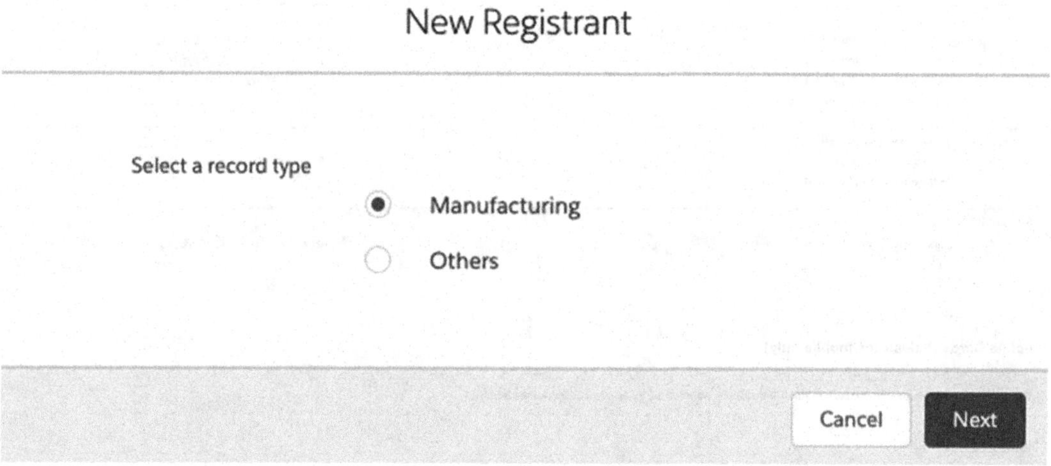

New Registrant

Select a record type

(•) Manufacturing

( ) Others

Cancel   Next

Figure 5-7. *Option to select a record type*

How Record Types Control Lightning Record Pages

As part of the Trailblazer Community, I have seen many questions from people wondering how record types and page layouts are connected in Lightning record pages. Here is my answer: a record type can control both page layout *and* Lightning record pages at the same time because they are separate components.

Are you still confused about how record types control Lightning pages and page layouts? Figure 5-8 is an architectural diagram that displays the connections among record types, Lightning record pages, and page layouts.

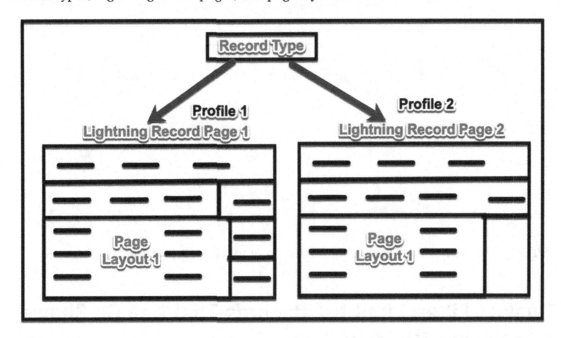

Figure 5-8. *How record type controls Lightning record pages and page layouts*

Figure 5-8 also shows that users in two different profiles can not only have the *same page layout* but also *different Lightning record pages* configured for their profiles—and vice versa!

Basically, in Lightning Experience, you use the Classic page layout as a component (Record Detail), which sits on top of the Lightning record page. This means both are separate Lightning components. Therefore, both are configurable at the object level.

After you create a Lightning record page, click the Activation button to assign the Lightning record page based on record types and profiles.

Figure 5-9 demonstrates how you can assign a Lightning record page to record types and profiles in Lightning App Builder.

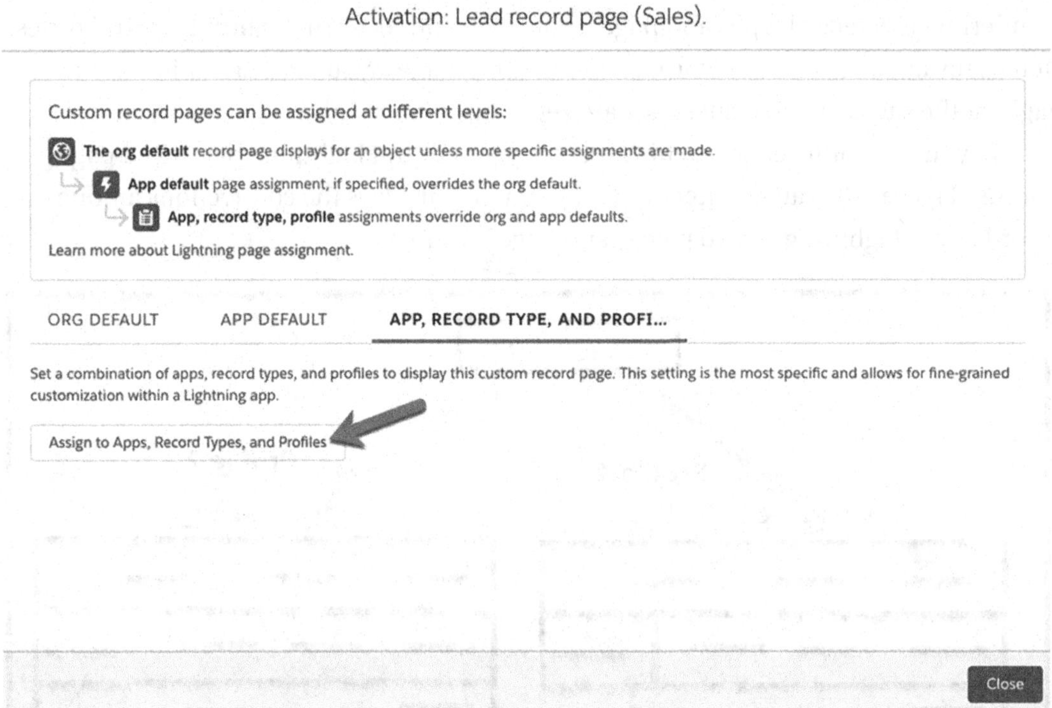

Activation: Lead record page (Sales).

Custom record pages can be assigned at different levels:

The **org default** record page displays for an object unless more specific assignments are made.

App default page assignment, if specified, overrides the org default.

App, record type, profile assignments override org and app defaults.

Learn more about Lightning page assignment.

ORG DEFAULT   APP DEFAULT   **APP, RECORD TYPE, AND PROFI...**

Set a combination of apps, record types, and profiles to display this custom record page. This setting is the most specific and allows for fine-grained customization within a Lightning app.

Assign to Apps, Record Types, and Profiles

Close

Figure 5-9. *Assigning a Lightning record page to record types and profiles*

Lookup Filter: Limit the Records That Can Be Shown in a Lookup Window

A lookup filter is one of the best tools to enrich data quality by enforcing data consistency. The filters limit fields and values displayed in a lookup dialog and, as a result, enforce access to valid values. The filter can be used when objects are in a lookup, master-detail, or hierarchical relationship.

Let's look at an example. Pamela Kline needs to restrict the Account Name field on opportunities by only allowing accounts with type Customer and by filtering out any other types of accounts.

To meet this requirement, Pamela performs the following steps.

1. She clicks Setup (gear icon) ➤ Setup ➤ Object Manager ➤ Opportunity ➤ Fields & Relationship ➤ Account Name and then clicks the Edit button.

2. Then, she navigates to the Lookup Filter section and clicks Show Filter Settings.

3. Pamela clicks the search icon and chooses Account Name. Then, she chooses Type and clicks Insert.

4. For Operator, she chooses equals.

5. For Value/Field, she chooses Value.

6. Then, she clicks the search icon and chooses Customer.

7. Next, she clicks Insert Suggested Criteria.

8. She makes sure the filter type is set to Required and the Active check box is selected, as shown in Figure 5-10.

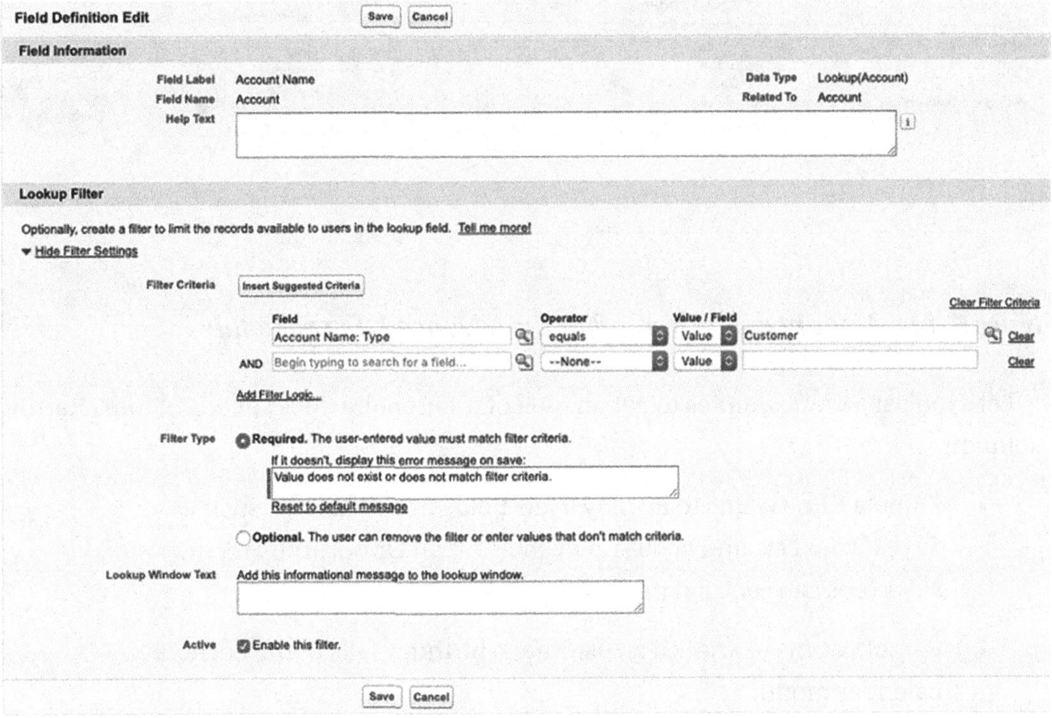

Figure 5-10. *Configuration options available for the lookup filter*

9.   When done, Pamela clicks the Save button.

Going forward, whenever a sales rep creates a new opportunity, Salesforce only shows the account whose type is Customer.

Formula Fields: Small Work, Big Impact

Formula fields are read-only fields that display values based on the expression of a formula that you define. When writing a formula's expression, you can refer to fields from the parent object, and it can go ten levels deeper. This means, for example, when writing a formula on an Opportunity object, you can refer to the account owner's email, as shown in Figure 5-11.

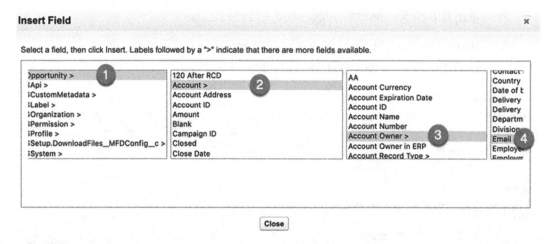

Figure 5-11. *Account owner's email in the Advanced Formula tab*

Let's look at a few examples to get an idea of different business needs before charting a solution.

- Pamela Kline wants to display a few fields from Account, such as Site, Industry, and Annual Revenue, on an Opportunity record so sales reps can see all data in one place.

- Pamela wants to know if a customer's birthday falls in the current calendar month.

- Pamela wants to create a clickable phone number field that dials a phone number automatically, using a dialing tool, when clicked.

- Carolina Lopez, a sales manager at GoC, wants to share a monthly installation with support agents but not the Loan Amount and Interest Rate fields, which reside in the Loan Details custom object.

The common objective in all the scenarios is to perform some automation. There are a few automation tools in Salesforce, and each one has unique features. For now, let's use formula fields to solve the business scenarios just presented. In the next chapter, however, several automation tools are examined.

When you reference a field from the parent object in a formula's expression, this type of formula is known as a *cross-object formula*, as shown in the screenshot in Figure 5-11. Using cross-object formulas, you can reference a field from the parent object (regardless of whether the relationship is lookup or master-detail).

You can create formula fields on standard or custom objects but not on an external object. As of the summer 2019 release, it is not possible to refer to fields on external objects in a formula. Any changes in the formula's expression are reflected automatically in the formula's field value.

Let's rejoin Pamela Kline, a system administrator at GoC, who has been given the task to display the annual revenue of a customer on the Contact record.

To meet this requirement, Pamela performs the following steps.

1. She selects Setup (gear icon) ➤ Setup ➤ Object Manager ➤ Contact ➤ Fields & Relationship and clicks the New button.

2. Then, she selects Formula as the data type and clicks the Next button.

3. She enters the field label Annual Revenue and chooses Currency as the data type, then clicks the Next button.

4. Pamela selects the Advanced Formula tab (1 in Figure 5-12) in the formula editor and then clicks Insert Field (2 in Figure 5-12). (The advanced formula editor contains many tools to create powerful formulas.)

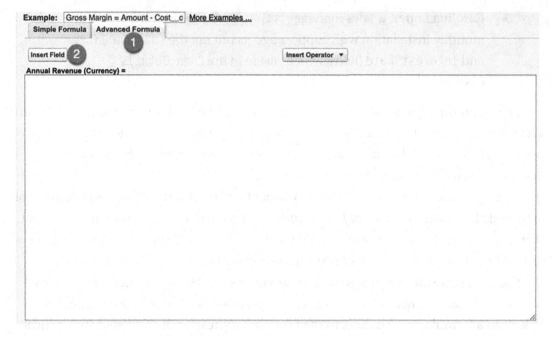

Figure 5-12. *Selecting the advanced formula editor*

5. Next, Pamela navigates to Contact (1 in Figure 5-13) ➤ Account
(2 in Figure 5-13) ➤ Annual Revenue (3 in Figure 5-13) and clicks
the Insert button (4 in Figure 5-13) to select the Annual Revenue
field from the Account object.

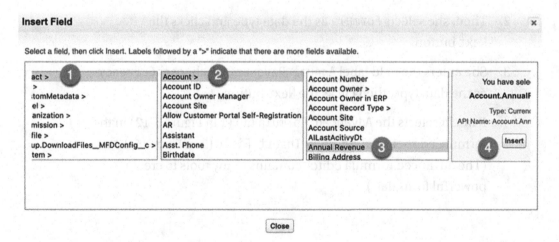

Figure 5-13. *Field selection in the formula editor*

6. When done, Pamela sees the formula's expression (1 in
   Figure 5-14) in the text area. She can also use the functions (2 in
   Figure 5-14) provided by Salesforce to write a complex formula.
   (Functions are convoluted operations that are pre-implemented
   by Salesforce.) After Pamela writes the formula, she clicks the
   Check Syntax button (3 in Figure 5-14) to confirm everything
   is in working order before saving. If there is a problem with her
   formula, the syntax checker warns her.

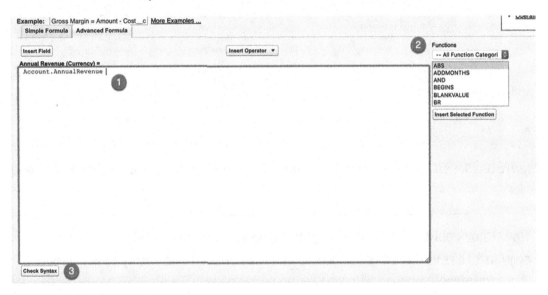

Figure 5-14. *Formula editor overview*

7. Pamela clicks the Next button, which redirects her to the page
   where she can establish field-level security. She does not make
   any changes but leaves all the default settings.

8. She clicks the Next button again, which allows her to add the
   formula field to her page layout.

9. Once done, she clicks the Save button.

Salesforce populates values in the Annual Revenue field (which is a formula field) for
all contacts in the Salesforce database. Remember, formula fields are Read Only fields,
and no one is allowed to edit their value. Formula fields can be used in list views to filter
data, as shown in Figure 5-15.

	NAME ↑	ACCOUNT NAME	ANNUAL REVENUE	MAILING COUNTRY	
1	Amelia Rudnicki	Extensive Enterprise	USD 1,143,275,254.95	United Kingdom	▾
2	Andy Smith	Universal Technologies	USD 139,000,000.00	United States	▾
3	Antoinette Barone	Red Packages	USD 116,000,000.00	United States	▾
4	Arthur Sawyer	Alvarez Electrical	USD 169,000,000.00	United States	▾
5	Brent Anctil	Electric Company	USD 124,000,000.00	United States	▾
6	Brett Blake	St Francis Hospital	USD 134,000,000.00	United States	▾
7	Chris Clay	St Francis Hospital	USD 134,000,000.00	United States	▾
8	Curtis Maughlin	West Airlines	USD 198,000,000.00	United States	▾
9	Desiree Gonzalez	Buck Foods	USD 131,000,000.00	United States	▾
10	Evan Everson	Allen Brothers Labs	USD 117,000,000.00	United States	▾
11	Fletcher Dickerson	George Mobile	USD 165,000,000.00	United States	▾
12	Floyd Mathews	Mckinney Foods Corp	USD 139,000,000.00	United States	▾
13	Frank Frederick	Allen Brothers Labs	USD 117,000,000.00	United States	▾
14	Gianna Martinez	Galaxy Corp	USD 1,143,275,254.95	United Kingdom	▾
15	Jannis Morris	Thatherton Fuels	USD 500,000,000.00	Australia	▾
16	Jocelyn Archila	ABC Telecom	USD 762,183,503.30	United Kingdom	▾
17	Jon Airaudi	Berk Hath Inc	USD 174,000,000.00	United States	▾
18	Kevin Adams	West Airlines	USD 198,000,000.00	United States	▾
19	Lisa Hernandez	Barrytron	USD 1,000,000,000.00	Australia	▾
20	Marlene Molina	General Services Corporation	USD 2,000,000,000.00	Australia	▾
21	Michael Toy	LexCorp	USD 1,143,275,254.95	United Kingdom	▾
22	Ned Hardy	Mccormick Telecoms Corporation	USD 200,000,000.00	United States	▾
23	Nick Bartlett	Glenn Media	USD 160,000,000.00	United States	▾

Figure 5-15. *All customers whose annual revenue is greater than US$100,000,000*

Tip   Check out the Salesforce documentation at `https://help.salesforce.com/articleView?id=customize_functions.htm&type=5` to learn more about formulas.

Roll-up Summary Field

A roll-up summary field is a custom field used to calculate values from related records and to display the value on a parent record. You can create roll-up summary fields on parent records only if the objects have a master-detail relationship.

For example, suppose there is a master-detail relationship between the College and Student custom objects, where College is the parent object and Student is a child object. Using a roll-up summary field, you can display the number of students currently active for each college record, as shown in Figure 5-16.

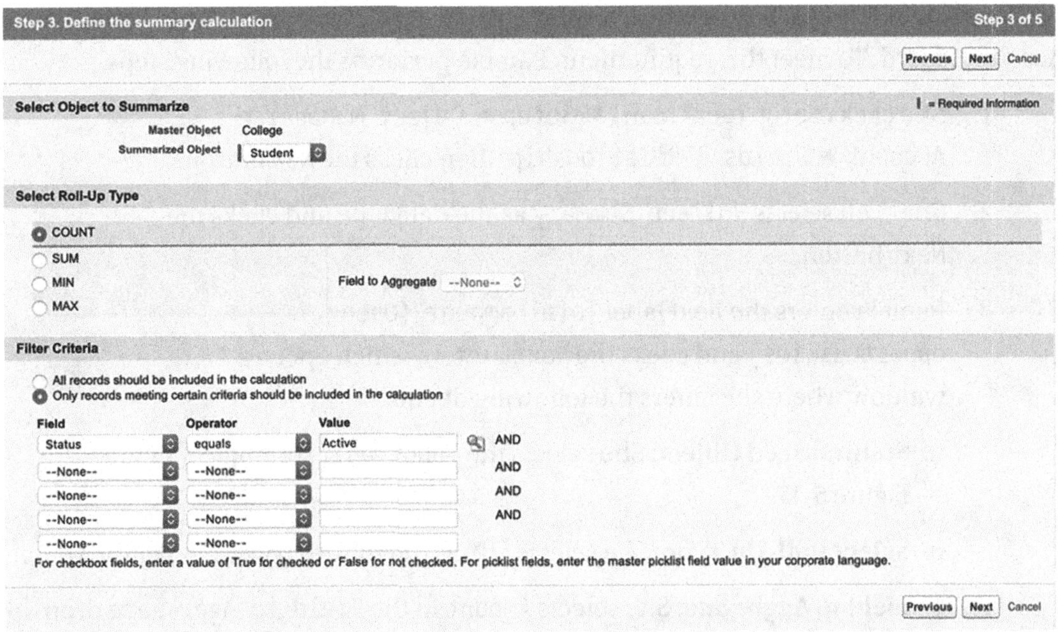

Figure 5-16. *Roll-up summary field for the College record to determine the number of active students*

A roll-up summary field contains different functions, such as the following.

- **COUNT**: This function is used to count the total number of related records.

- **SUM**: This function is used to sum values in the related record's field. You select the field from the Field to Aggregate drop-down. Only currency, number, and percent fields are available for selection.

- **MIN**: This function is used to find the minimum value on a field. You select the field from the Field to Aggregate drop-down across all related records. Only currency, date, date/time, number, and percent fields are available for selection.

- **MAX**: This function is used to find the maximum value on a field. You select the field from the Field to Aggregate drop-down across all related records. Only the currency, date, date/time, number, and percent fields are available for selection.

Let's rejoin Pamela. She needs to display Sum of Open Opportunities Amount in the Account record. To meet this requirement, Pamela performs the following steps.

1. She clicks Setup (gear icon) ➤ Setup ➤ Object Manager ➤ Account ➤ Fields & Relationship, then clicks the New button.

2. She then selects Roll-up Summary as the data type and clicks the Next button.

3. Pamela enters the field label Total amount (Open opportunities) and clicks the Next button, which opens a window where she enters the following details.

   a. **Summarized Object**: She selects the Opportunities object (1 in Figure 5-17).

   b. **Select Roll-Up Type**: She selects SUM as the roll-up type (2 in Figure 5-17).

   c. **Field to Aggregate**: She selects Amount in the Field to Aggregate drop-down (3 in Figure 5-17).

   d. **Filter Criteria**: She selects "Only records meeting certain criteria should be included in the calculation" (3 in Figure 5-17) and then she selects Closed ➤ equals to False (4 in Figure 5-17) as filter criteria. In the end, her screen looks like Figure 5-17.

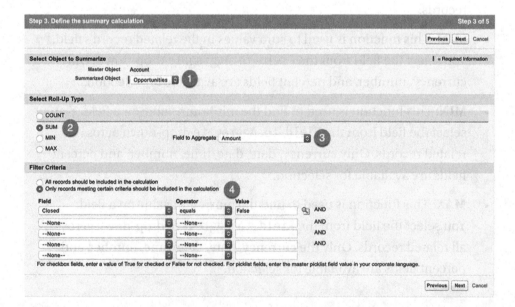

Figure 5-17. *Roll-up summary field to summarize the open opportunities amount*

4.   When done, Pamela clicks the Next button, which redirects her to
     the page where she can establish field-level security. She doesn't
     make any changes but leaves them as default values.

5.   She clicks the Next button, which allows her to add the roll-up
     summary field to her page layout.

6.   Pamela clicks the Save button.

Salesforce now populates the "Total amount (Open opportunities)" field values
for all opportunities. Remember, roll-up summary fields are Read Only fields; no one is
allowed to edit their value.

Tip   Check out the Salesforce documentation at https://help.salesforce.
com/articleView?id=fields_about_roll_up_summary_fields.
htm&type=s to discover hidden gems regarding the roll-up summary field.

Validation Rules

Validation rules help organizations improve the quality of data by verifying that the data
entered by users meets business standards. If the data don't meet the standards, users
get a prompt with an error message to fix the error, as shown in Figure 5-18.

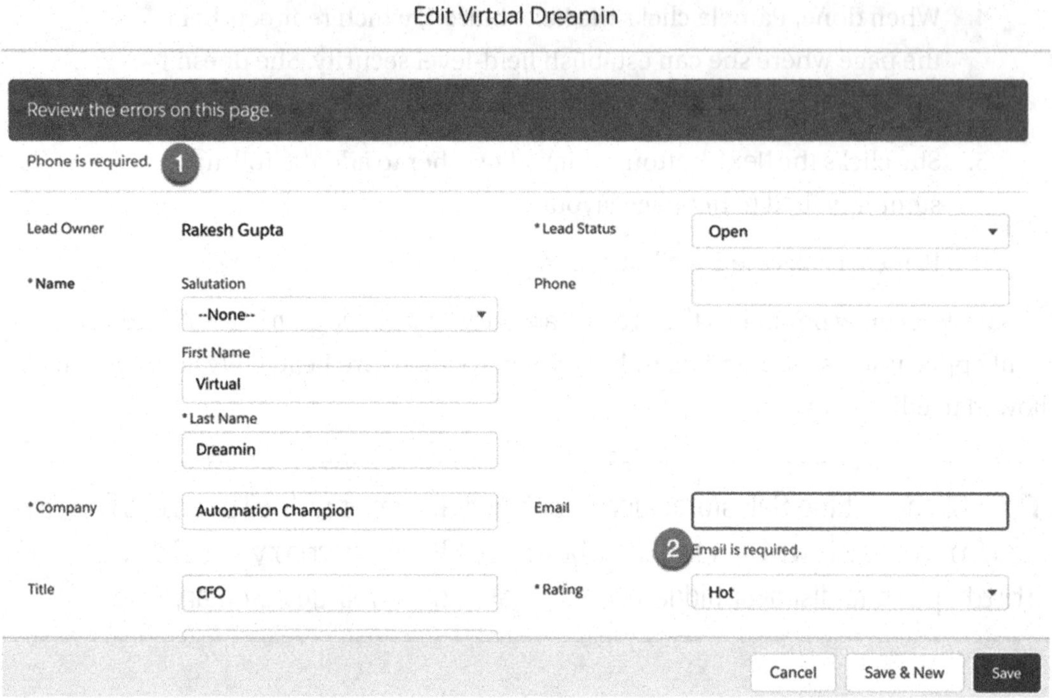

Figure 5-18. *Validation rules error messages*

A validation rule can contain a formula that evaluates the data in one or more fields and returns a value that is either True or False, where true means no error and false means there is an error. You can display the validation rule error message either at the top of the page (1 in Figure 5-18) or next to the field (2 in Figure 5-18).

Pamela Kline has been tasked to validate that an account's annual revenue is not negative and does not exceed US$1,000,000,000. To meet this requirement, Pamela performs the following steps.

1. She clicks Setup (gear icon) ➤ Setup ➤ Object Manager ➤ Account ➤ Validation Rules, then clicks the New button. This opens a window where she enters the following details.

    a. **Rule Name**: Pamela types Annual_revenue_cannt_be_greater_than_1bn.

    b. **Description**: She writes some meaningful text so other developers and administrators can easily understand why this custom field was created.

    c. **Error Condition Formula**: She uses the following formula.

```
OR(
    AnnualRevenue < 0,
    AnnualRevenue > 1000000000
)
```

d. **Error Message**: She enters the following message: Annual revenue cannot exceed 1 billion.

e. **Error Location**: She selects the Annual Revenue field.

Her screen looks like Figure 5-19.

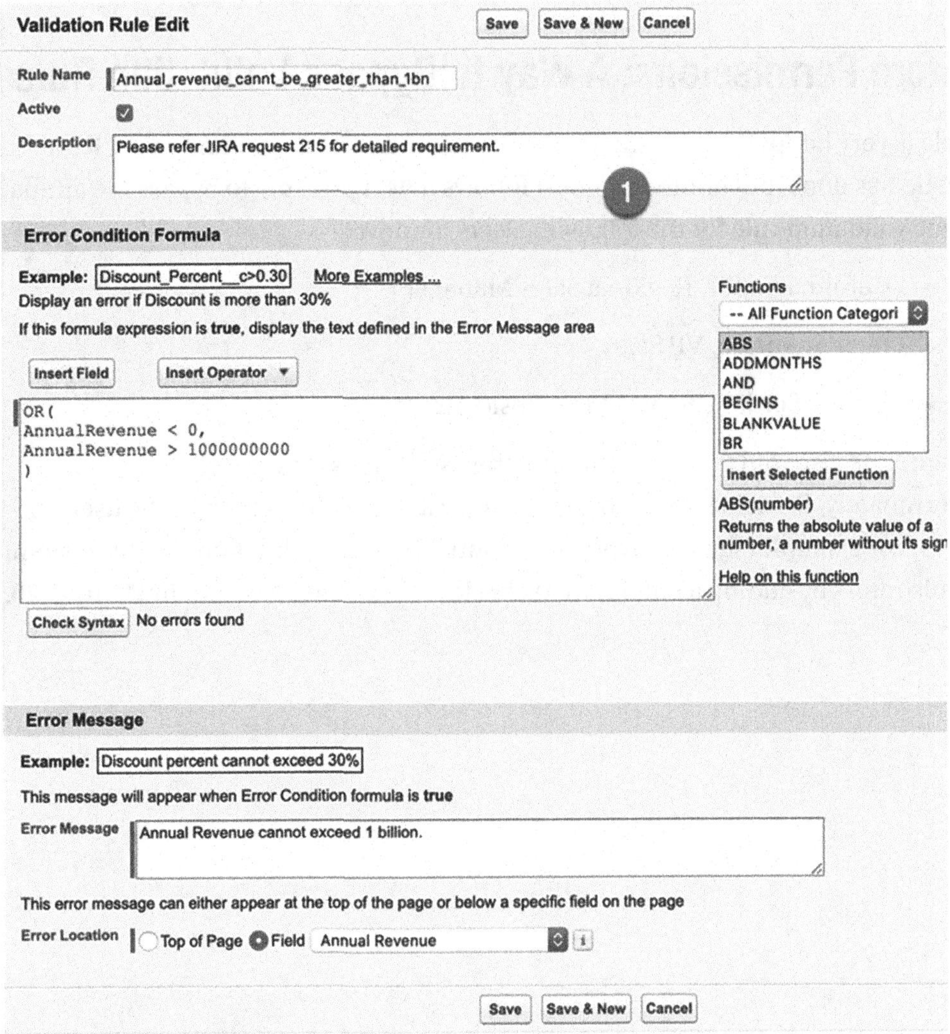

Figure 5-19. A validation rule to check annual revenue

2.   Pamela clicks the Save button.

Going forward, if users update their annual revenue with an amount greater than US$1,000,000,000, they get an error message and must fix the error before they can save the record.

Tip   Check out the Salesforce documentation at `https://help.salesforce.com/articleView?id=fields_useful_field_validation_formulas.htm&type=5` to find examples of validation rules.

Custom Permissions: A Way to Bypass Validation Rules

Pamela is very happy. She just got an appreciation email from her manager for all the work she has done, but another request follows it. Is it possible to bypass the annual revenue validation rule for the following users for now?

- Carolina Lopez, Regional Sales Manager

- Jerry Shannon, VP Sales

- Donna Serdula, Senior Vice President

Pamela is also told that, in the future, the list of users may grow!

Fortunately, Pamela knows how to bypass validation rules for specific users or profiles. For example, she can bypass the annual revenue validation rule for system administrators by adding a condition to check their profile, as shown in Figure 5-20.

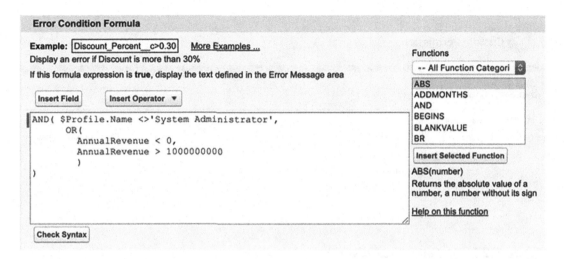

Figure 5-20. *Bypass a validation rule for a system administrator's profile*

Pamela wonders whether there is a better way to handle this task. She doesn't want to modify the validation rule every time she is required to add a new user to the bypass validation list.

Custom permissions to rescue! Pamela learned recently that, by using custom permissions, she can grant users access to custom apps. In Salesforce, she can use custom permissions to check which users can access a certain functionality. Using custom permissions, she can bypass validation rules, formula fields, Process Builder, Apex triggers, and so on. Custom permissions let her define access checks that can be assigned to users via profiles or permission sets.

To meet this requirement, Pamela performs the following steps.

1. She clicks Setup (gear icon) ➤ Setup ➤ PLATFORM TOOLS ➤ Custom Code ➤ Custom Permissions, and clicks the New button.

2. She creates a custom permission, as shown in Figure 5-21.

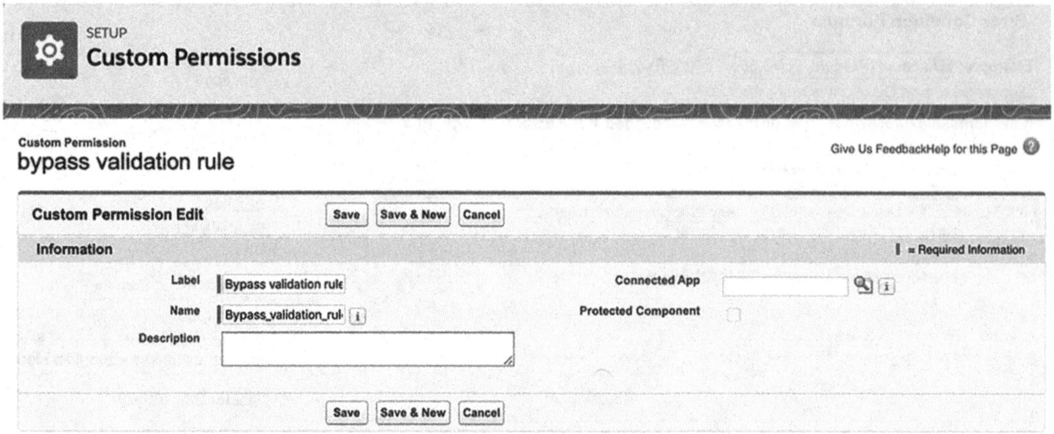

Figure 5-21. *A custom permission*

3. She creates a permission set (Bypass validation rule) and assigns it, as shown in Figure 5-22).

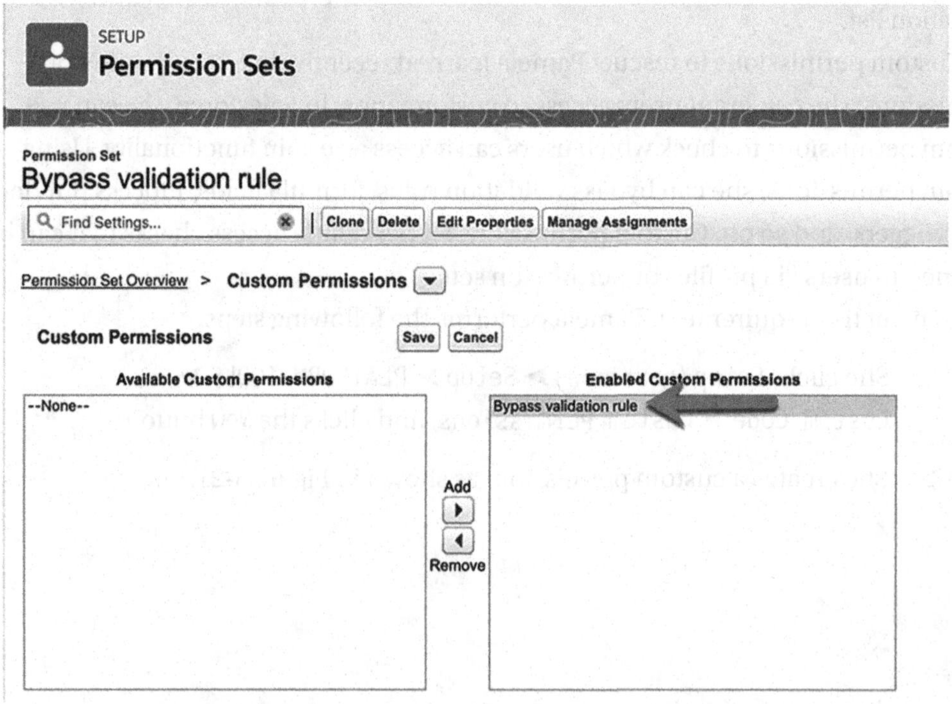

Figure 5-22. *Assigning custom permission to a permission set*

4. Next, Pamela modifies the annual revenue validation rule to add a custom permission check. To do so, she navigates to Setup (gear icon) ➤ Setup ➤ Object Manager ➤ Account ➤ Validation Rules and edits the annual revenue validation rule.

5. She modifies the formula as follows.

```
AND(NOT($Permission.Bypass_validation_rule), OR(
      AnnualRevenue < 0,
      AnnualRevenue > 1000000000
      )
)
```

6. To select the custom permission, she clicks Insert Field (1 in Figure 5-23) and then $Permission ➤ Bypass_validation_rule ➤ Insert (2 in Figure 5-23).

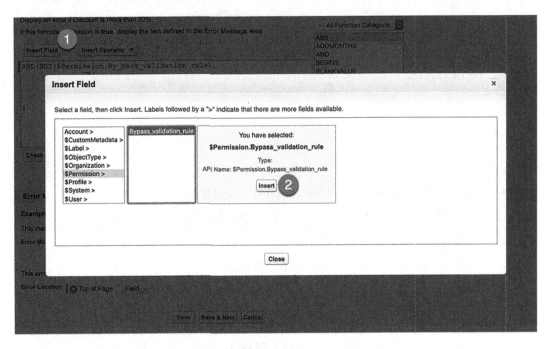

Figure 5-23. *Selecting a custom permission*

7. Pamela clicks the Save button.

Pamela assigns the Bypass Validation Rule permission to users Carolina Lopez, Jerry Shannon, and Donna Serdula. And that's it! Now, the validation rule has been bypassed for these users. In the future, if Pamela wants to bypass a validation rule for other users, all she must do is assign the permission set to those users.

Points to Remember

- The following picklist fields are not available for record types because they are controlled by sales processes, lead processes, support processes, and solution processes, respectively.

    - `Opportunity Stage`

    - `Case Status`

    - `Solution Status`

    - `Lead Status`

- The following campaign member picklist fields are not available for record types.

    - `Status`

    - `Salutation`

    - `Lead Source`

- It is not possible to deactivate a record type if it is in use by the `Email-to-Case` or `On-Demand Email-to-Case` routing email address.

- Lookup filters improve user efficiency by controlling the number of available records in a lookup search dialog.

- In Lightning Experience, a lookup filter doesn't work if a field referenced in the filtered lookup isn't added to the page layout.

- It is not possible to refer to cross-object formulas in roll-up summary fields.

- Salesforce allows a maximum of ten unique relationships per object in cross-object formulas.

- Formula fields can comprise up to 3900 characters, including spaces, return characters, and comments. If your formula needs more characters, create separate formula fields and reference them in another formula field.

- It is not possible to reference long text areas, encrypted fields, or description fields in formulas.

- It is not possible to delete fields referenced in formulas. Remove the field from the formula before deleting it.

- When you delete a child record from a roll-up summary field, Salesforce *does not recalculate the value of the field*. Select the `Force a mass recalculation` option on the edit page of the roll-up summary field to recalculate the value manually.

- When one validation rule fails, Salesforce continues to check other validation rules on that field, or other fields, on the page and displays all error messages at once.

- It is possible to use roll-up summary fields in validation rules. However, you cannot use a roll-up summary field as a location to display an error message because roll-up summary fields do not display on edit pages.

- You can create custom permissions only in the Enterprise edition or higher.

Hands-on Exercises

The following exercises give you more practice with the platform, which ultimately will help you gain mastery of it and assist you in preparing for the certification examination. Remember, these are hands-on exercises, and you can find the answers at the back of the book in the appendix, but try to implement them in your Salesforce org, which is the primary goal of doing them.

1. Configure business processes on Lead in such a way that when users create a lead for North America or Asia Pacific, they only see the following values on lead status.

   a. Lead status for North America

      New
      Suspect
      Interested
      Working
      Qualified (Converted)

   b. Lead status on Asia Pacific

      New
      Open
      Qualified (Converted)

2. Configure the Lead Lightning record page to include the following components.

   a. Activities

   b. Chatter

   c. Related List Quick Links

   Assign them to the North America record type only.

3. Dennis Williams, a system administrator at GoC, must meet the following requirements for the Account Name field on the Contact object.

   a. The account name lookup dialog should only display accounts that have Mumbai as the site name.

   b. The previous constraint should not apply to users with a system administrator profile.

   How would you instruct Dennis to fulfill these tasks?

4. Business managers at GoC found that sales reps are creating opportunities for competitors' accounts. As an app builder, how can you restrict sales reps from selecting competitors' accounts while creating a new opportunity?

5. Create a custom field (data type: Lookup Relationship) on the Opportunity object with the Contact object. This should allow users to select a contact when creating a new opportunity.

6. Keeping the previous requirement in mind, configure the lookup in such a way that it only displays the contacts related to the account with which the opportunity is associated!

7. Dennis wants to implement opportunity management at GoC, but he is a bit confused by one of the tasks. Because you now have a better understanding of record sharing, please help him select the appropriate sharing architecture to fulfill the following requirements.

    a. When the opportunity amount is greater than US$1,000,000 make sure the Next Step field is required.

    b. However, make sure it doesn't apply to the following users.

        • Jerry Shannon, VP Sales

        • Users with a system administrator profile

        • Users with the sales rep-APAC profile

8. Help Dennis write the correct formula for the following tasks (formula field).

    a. Create a custom field that determines the telephone country code of a contact based on the shipping country on the shipping address.

    b. Create a custom drop-down on a contact's preferred phone with the values Home Phone, Asst. Phone, Other Phone, and Phone. Next, create a formula field that shows the phone number based on what the user provided in the Preferred Phone field.

    c. Create a formula field that displays the first three characters of a name and year from the Date of Birth field separated by a dash.

    d. Create a formula field on Account that displays the ratings Hot, Warm, or Cold based on the following criteria.

- Annual revenue should be greater than US$50,000,000.

- The billing country should contain United States, US, USA, CANADA, CA, MEXICO, or MX.

- If the account fulfills these two requests and belongs to type Reseller, Integrator, or Partner, then the rating should be Hot; type Prospect or Investor, then the rating should be Warm; for everything else, then the rating should be Cold.

e. Create a formula field on the Opportunity object to calculate the number of days since an opportunity with an account was opened. If the opportunity is closed (either won or lost), this field should be blank.

f. Create a formula field on the Contact object that displays the month as a text string instead of a number from the Date of Birth field.

g. Create a formula field on Lead to calculate the number of days the lead has been open. If the lead is qualified or unqualified, then the formula field should be blank.

9. Help Dennis to write the correct formula for the following tasks (validation rule).

a. Create a validation rule to prompt an error message to users if a quote line-item discount exceeds 23%.

b. If the Phone field on the Contact object doesn't contain ten digits, it displays an error message to the users.

c. Create the custom field Delivery Date on the Opportunity object. Now write a validation rule to make sure that this custom field must be populated if an opportunity stage is Closed Won or Negotiation/Review.

d. Write a validation rule to make sure the close date of an opportunity cannot be in the past.

e. Write a validation rule to make sure that users are only allowed to update the opportunity if they have added products to the opportunity.

f. Write a validation rule that prevents sales reps from changing Opportunity Stage to anything other than Closed Won or Closed Lost, after Opportunity Stage is set to Closed Won or Closed Lost.

g. Write a validation rule to make sure the probability of a lost opportunity is set to 0%.

10. Create a custom field on Account to display the maximum amount from the related opportunity that is marked Closed Won.

Summary

This chapter covered record types and how they include pages in Salesforce Classic vs. Lightning Experience. It also studied different mechanisms to improve data quality using filter lookups and validation rules and reviewed roll-up summary and formula fields by examining a few examples. The next chapter dives into how to automate business processes using out-of-the-box automation tools.

CHAPTER 6

Automating Business Processes

Abstract

Chapter 5 covered record types, offered an in-depth overview of data improvement tools such as lookup filters, formula fields, and roll-up summary fields, and looked at validation rules with real-life examples.

This chapter provides an overview of the Salesforce Flow life cycle and takes a close look at Salesforce Flow Designer, offering a few use cases. The chapter also closely examines the approval process with a real-life example.

Introduction to Salesforce Flow

Salesforce Flow is a drag-and-drop interface that allows you to automate business processes by using clicks, not code. Using Salesforce Flow, you can undertake a few actions: create, update, and delete records; send email; submit records for approval; send notifications to Salesforce mobile; automate Quip; post a message to chatter; make an HTTPS callout, and create a guided process and make it available to end users.

Salesforce Flow can run automatically without using any manual intervention. It can interact with Salesforce objects and can invoke Apex classes (an Apex class implements @InvocableMethod annotation). Using Salesforce Flow, you can create a series of screens to take user input to collect the data and process them in Salesforce based on your logic.

Let's meet up with Pamela Kline again, who has just received a new request from her manager: add new users automatically to a public group named Company Announcements.

Pamela has several options for fulfilling this request.

- **Apex trigger**: This option requires Apex programming skills. Pamela writes a test class to deploy the Apex trigger into production, which is a time-consuming undertaking, to say the least.

```
trigger addintoPublicgroup on User (after insert) {
  for (User AddUser: trigger.new)
   {
             If (AddUser.Isactive == True)
        {
       // Your logic;
}
     }
    }
```

- **Salesforce Flow**: This option uses a record-triggered Flow, as shown in Figure 6-1.

- In Record-Triggered Flow, Pamela would write the logic to add people to the public group.

- Logic executes whenever a new user record gets created.

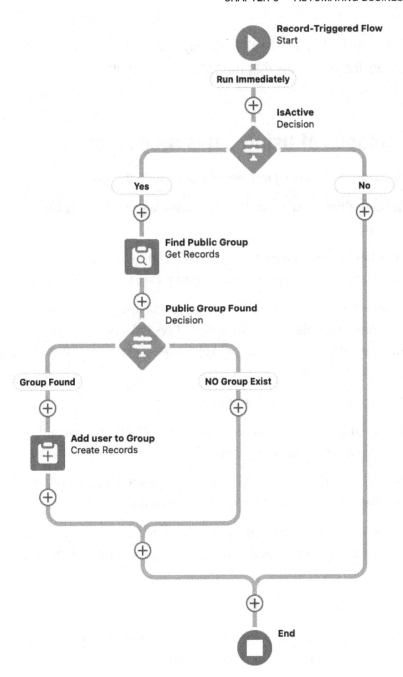

Figure 6-1. *A Salesforce Flow solution*

Note   A flow can be triggered automatically either as a record-triggered flow or as a scheduled-triggered flow that runs at a specified time.

The Advantages of Using Salesforce Flow

The benefits of using Salesforce Flow over Apex include the following.

- The flow allows you to automate a business process using clicks, not code.

- It does not require coding skills. Without knowing Apex code, you can develop a flow to automate business processes.

- It allows you to make an HTTPS callout, which can be very helpful for connecting Salesforce with external systems. For example, automatically update currency rates once a day, make callouts to get the weather forecast, and so forth.

- Non-developers can easily maintain it.

- Because it is not code, you don't need to write test classes (although there are a few exceptions to this).

- You can also use your flow skills when implementing Einstein Bots, Next Best Action, Flow Orchestrator, and so on.

One of the few downsides of using Flow, however, is that you can make changes directly in an organization's production org, just like any other configuration. Ouch!

The Salesforce Flow Life Cycle

Salesforce Flow Designer is a tool for creating, configuring, and managing flows. It is used to define business logic for your flows without having to write a single line of code. It has three parts.

- **Design**: Salesforce Flow Designer is a tool to create flows, configure screens, and define business logic for your flows without writing a single line of code.

- **Administration**: After you create a flow, you can manage it, edit its properties, grant flow access to profiles, activate it, deactivate it, delete it, save it as a new version or a new flow, or just run an existing flow.

- **Runtime**: You can run an active flow from a custom button, link, Flow action, Salesforce page, and more. If it is an autolaunched flow, then it can be executed through Process Builder or run at a specified time.

An Overview of Salesforce Flow Designer

Salesforce Flow Designer is a tool that allows you to create flows, configure screens, and define business logic for your flows without requiring a single line of code. Flow Designer's user interface has several different functional parts (see Figure 6-2).

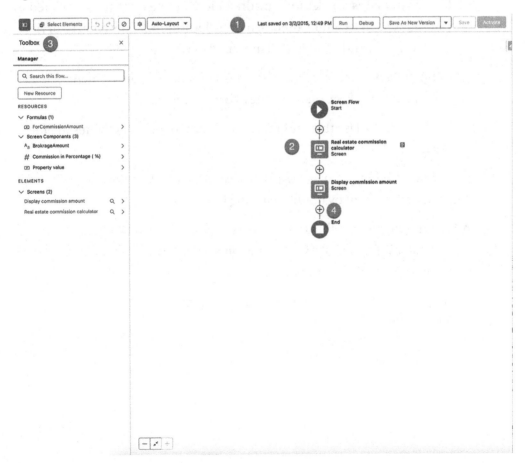

Figure 6-2. *Salesforce Flow Designer*

1. **The button bar**: You can use the Save, Save As New Version, Activate, Debug, Run, Undo, and Redo buttons to perform specific activities.

    a. **Save**: Use this option to save your flow.

    b. **Save As**: Use this option to clone a flow or create a new version of the flow.

    c. **Activate**: Use this option to activate the flow.

    d. **Debug**: Use this option to see the real-time details of what your flow does and why it is not working. Set input variables and restart the flow at any time to debug a different branch.

    e. **Run**: Use this option to run the most recent version of the flow you are working on.

    f. **Flow Properties**: Click the screwdriver icon to see information related to your flow, such as name, unique name, description, flow type, interview label, version, and created and modified dates.

    g. **Copy** or **Paste**: Use this option to copy and paste a flow element (such as Screen, Create Records, and Decision) one at a time.

    h. **Undo** or **Redo**: Use this option to undo or redo recent activities in Flow Designer.

2. **The Flow Designer**: You can use this area to design your flow. You can edit any element by double-clicking it.

3. **Add Elements**: This is the area where you can find all the element types available for your flow. Click the plus icon to select an element from the list of options Salesforce provides.

4. **Manager**: The Manager tab contains all the elements and resources added to the flow.

Different Ways to Launch a Flow

After you are done with flow development, the next task is to distribute the flow so business users can use it. There are several ways business users can run the flow.

- Flow Component – Lightning Home Page

- Flow Component – Lightning Record Page

- Flow Component – Lightning App Page

- Custom button or link

- Quick action

- Utility bar

- Subflow

- Login low

- Experience cloud site

- Automatically at a specified time

- Record is Created

- Record is Updated

- Record is Deleted

- APIs

- Apex

- Visualforce page

- Lightning web component

- Lightning component

This list is not exhaustive. Now that we've looked at the nuts and bolts of Salesforce Flow, let's explore how you can use it in real life.

Use Case 1: Mortgage Broker Commission Calculator

At GoC, mortgage brokers often get confused about their commission for a given deal. They are having a hard time calculating the commission correctly. Pamela Kline wants to create an application that allows mortgage brokers to calculate their commissions.

On the very first screen, she wants to allow mortgage brokers to enter the property's value (in dollars) and the commission (as a percentage), as shown in Figure 6-3.

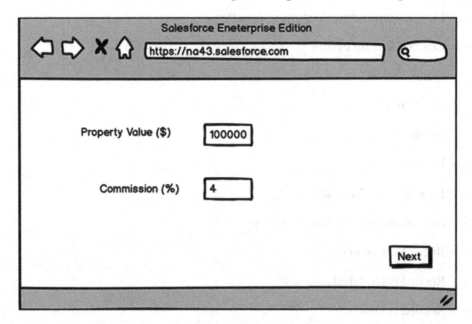

Figure 6-3. *Mortgage broker commission calculator*

On the next screen, Pamela wants to display the commission amount (in dollars), as shown in Figure 6-4.

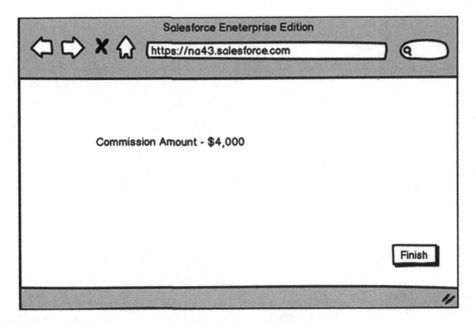

Figure 6-4. *Calculator displays the commission amount*

Pamela does this by performing the following steps.

1. She navigates to Setup (gear icon) ➤ Setup ➤ Process Automation ➤ Flow.

2. She then clicks the New Flow button, which opens a pop-up, where she selects the Screen Flow option and then clicks the Create button. These actions open Salesforce Flow Designer.

3. Pamela navigates to the Elements tab and drags and drops the Screen element to Salesforce Flow Designer, which opens a Screen element window.

4. She enters the **Mortgage broker commission calculator** label and adds a description. Then, she uses the Configure Frame section to control the appearance of the header and footer. Within the Control Navigation section, she selects the Next or Finish option only, as shown in Figure 6-5.

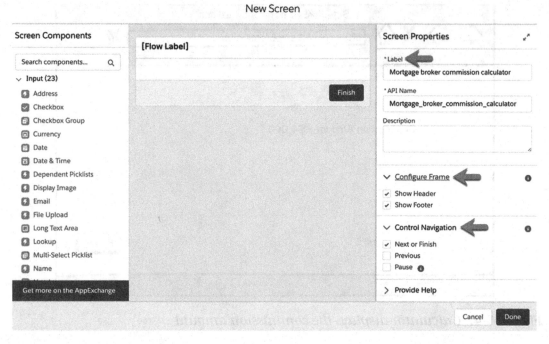

Figure 6-5. *Configure Screen element properties*

5. Next, Pamela uses the Screen element to display the fields so that mortgage brokers can enter the property value and their commission as a percentage. She drags and drops the Currency field onto the Screen element and configures it by clicking the Currency field to configure its settings by entering the following information.

    a. **Label**: Pamela enters the label for the input currency field. In this case, she enters **Property value ($)** as the label.

    b. **API Name**: This field autopopulates based on the label.

    c. **Require**: She selects this check box to make the field required.

    d. **Default Value**: Users can enter a default value for this field that would prepopulate the value for the component. For this requirement, Pamela leaves the field empty.

e. **Decimal Places**: Pamela uses this field to control the number of digits to the right of the decimal point. She knows the number of digits can't exceed 17.

f. **Set Component Visibility**: Pamela uses this section to control component visibility based on the flow's attributes.

g. **Validate Input**: Here, Pamela knows she can provide a formula that evaluates whether the value that is entered is valid. She also knows she should add an error message to display if the value input is invalid.

h. **Provide Help**: Pamela knows she can use this field to give her users more context with this screen component.

In the end, Pamela's screen component looks like Figure 6-6.

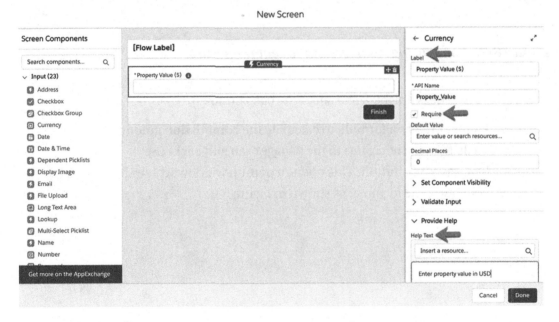

Figure 6-6. *Configure currency component properties*

6. Then, Pamela adds the Number field to allow mortgage brokers to enter their commission as a percentage. In the end, her flow looks like Figure 6-7.

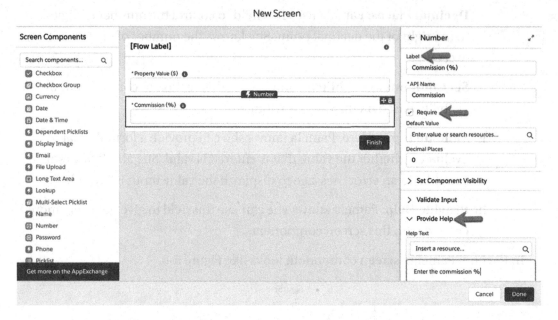

Figure 6-7. *Configuring number component properties*

7. When she is finished, she clicks the Done button.

8. Pamela creates a formula to calculate the commission amount. To do this, she navigates to the Manager tab and clicks the New Resource button. This opens a pop-up window where she configures the formula, as shown in Figure 6-8.

New Resource

* Resource Type

Formula ▼

* API Name

forCommissionAmount

Description

↻

* Data Type

Currency ▼

Decimal Places

0

* Formula

Insert a resource...   🔍

{!Property_Value}*{!Commission}/100

↻

Cancel   **Done**

Figure 6-8. *Formula to calculate commission amount*

{!Property_value} and {!Commission} are screen input fields Pamela created in steps 5 and 6.

9.   When she is finished, she clicks the Done button.

10.   The next task is for her to display the commission amount on the screen. For that, Pamela drags and drops the Screen element from Elements to Flow Designer. This opens a Screen element window, where Pamela enters the name: **Display mortgage commission amount.** She uses the Configure Frame section to control the appearance of the header and footer. Within the Control Navigation section, Pamela selects the Next or Finish option only.

11.   She navigates to the Screen Component section and double-clicks Display Text, which is available in the Display section.

12. In the screen overlay preview pane, Pamela clicks the Display
     Text field to configure its settings by entering the API name. From
     the Display Text drop-down, Pamela selects the formula she
     created in step 8. The final product looks like Figure 6-9.

New Screen

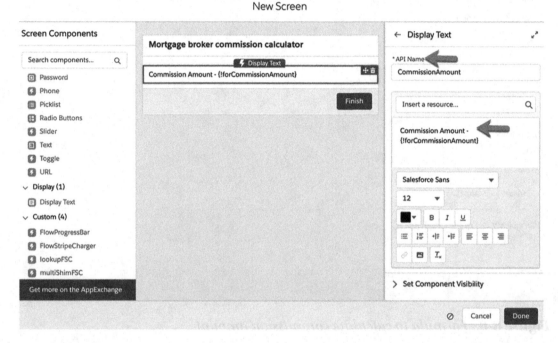

Figure 6-9. *Configure the second screen to display the commission amount.*

13. When she is finished, Pamela clicks the Done button.

Connecting the Flow Elements

So far, Pamela has created two screens: one for getting input from the mortgage broker
and the other for displaying the commission amount in dollars. Pamela needs to connect
both elements so that, at runtime, the flow can decide the order of execution of the
elements.

1. To do this, in the Start element, Pamela finds the node at the
    bottom and drags the node to the target element, as shown in
    Figure 6-10.

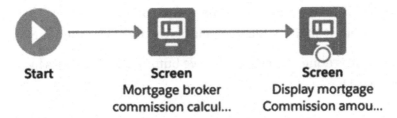

Figure 6-10. *Connecting the flow elements*

2.   Pamela clicks the Save button and enters **Mortgage broker commission calculator** as the name to save the flow.

3.   Pamela activates the flow by clicking the `Activate` button.

Activating a Version of a Flow

When users activate a flow, Salesforce does not allow them to modify the activated flow. At this point, users have two options.

- Create a new flow by cloning the activated flow.

- Modify the activated flow, save it as a new version, and then modify it. When users are done with modification, they can activate the new version of the flow.

Users can have multiple versions of a flow, but they can activate only one version of a flow at a time. From the flow detail page, Salesforce allows users to activate or deactivate one version of a flow. Users click the `Activate` link next to the version of the flow they want.

Displaying a Flow from the Salesforce Home Page

At this point, Pamela has created and activated a flow. The next step is to distribute it so that mortgage brokers can use it. She wants to place this application on the Salesforce home page. She does this by performing the following steps.

1.   She edits the Salesforce home page by navigating to App Builder.

2.   She drags and drops the flow component onto the page.

3.   Next, she selects the flow she wants to display: Mortgage broker commission calculator.

4. She can also select the layout (one or two columns) and set component visibility, which Pamela leaves as the default value.

5. When she is done, she clicks the Save button. Her flow looks like Figure 6-11.

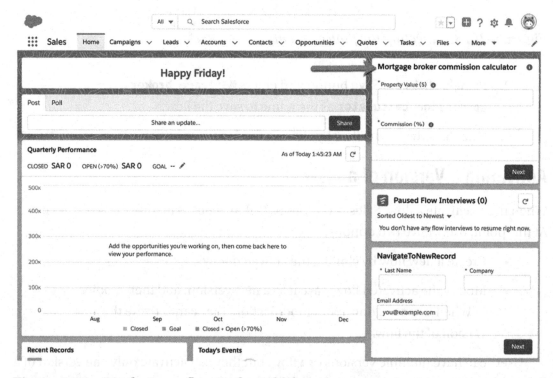

Figure 6-11. *Displaying a flow in the Salesforce home page*

I hope you now have a better understanding of how to create a flow and activate it for business users.

Use Case 2: Delete Unqualified Leads

Pamela Kline has received a task from her manager. Whenever a lead is updated as Closed - Not Converted, it must be deleted. This helps GoC maintain a clean database.

A flow can be invoked manually using buttons, links, or actions. In Pamela's situation, she needs to call the flow automatically whenever a lead is updated to unqualified and then delete the record. In such cases, you need to use a record-triggered flow. Figure 6-12 shows the process flow diagram for the new business requirement.

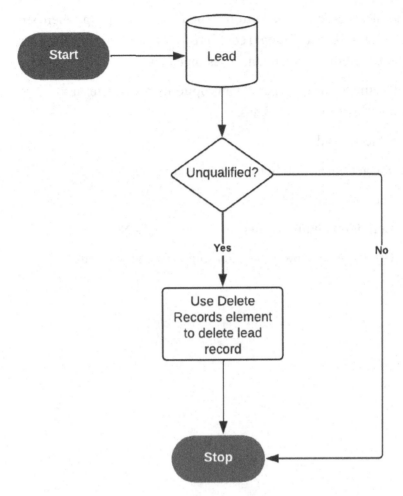

Figure 6-12. *Process flow diagram for use case 2*

Now that you see why two tools are needed to solve the task, let's plow through the following steps.

1. A record-triggered flow is used to delete the Lead record based on the record updated by the logged-in user.

To solve the task, Pamela performs the following steps using Salesforce Flow.

1. She makes sure to add Unqualified as a value in the Lead Status field.

2. Then she navigates to Setup (gear icon) ➤ Setup ➤ Process Automation ➤ Flow.

3. She clicks the New Flow button, which opens a pop-up, where she selects the Record-Triggered Flow option, and then clicks the Create button, which opens Salesforce Flow.

4. Select the Record-Triggered Flow option, click Create, and configure the flow as follows.

    a. Object: Lead

    b. Trigger the Flow When: A record is updated

    c. Set Entry Criteria

    d. Condition Requirements: Status = Closed – Not Converted

    e. Optimize the Flow for Action and Related Records

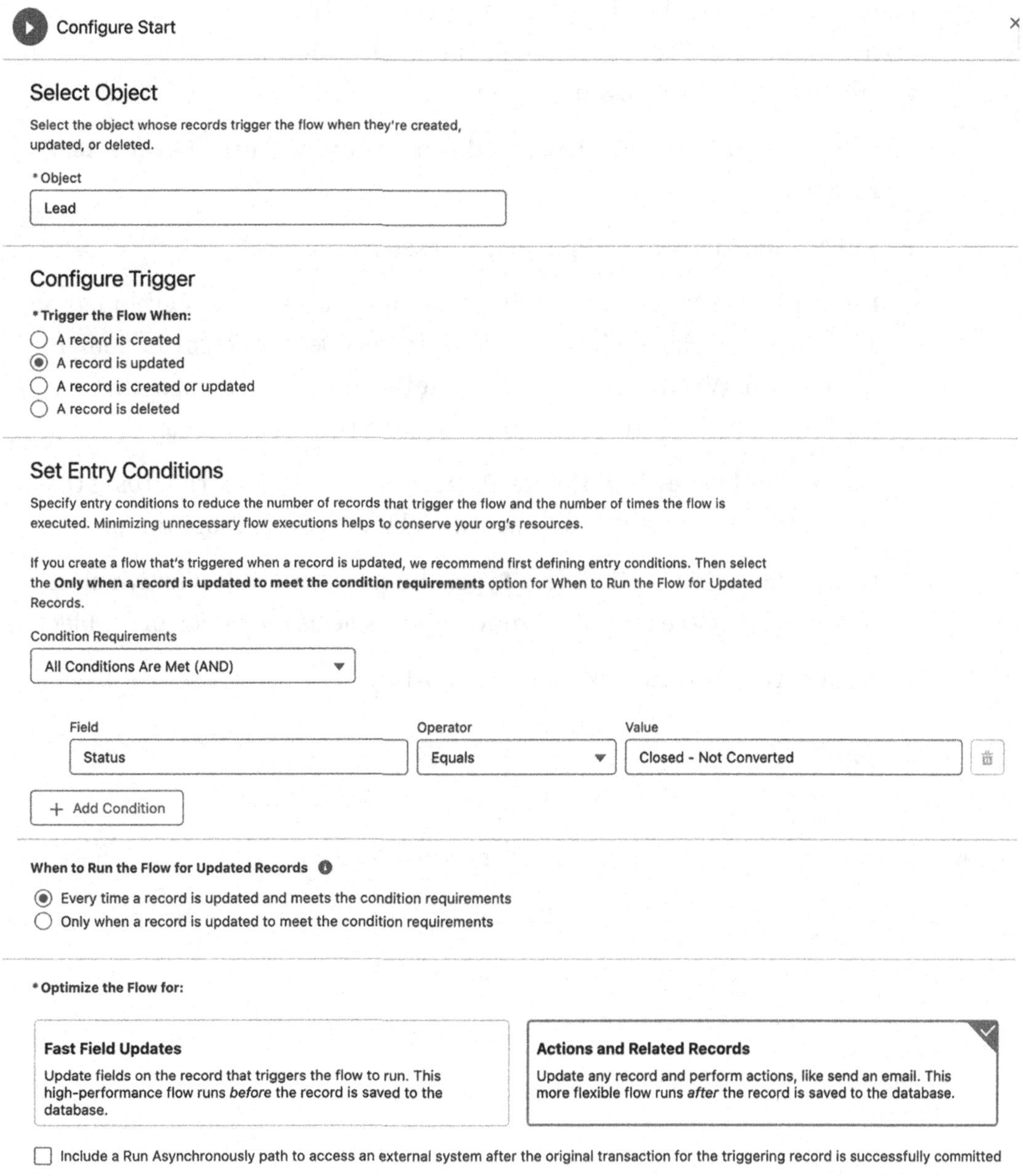

▶ Configure Start   ✕

Select Object

Select the object whose records trigger the flow when they're created,
updated, or deleted.

* Object

| Lead |

Configure Trigger

* Trigger the Flow When:

○ A record is created
◉ A record is updated
○ A record is created or updated
○ A record is deleted

Set Entry Conditions

Specify entry conditions to reduce the number of records that trigger the flow and the number of times the flow is
executed. Minimizing unnecessary flow executions helps to conserve your org's resources.

If you create a flow that's triggered when a record is updated, we recommend first defining entry conditions. Then select
the Only when a record is updated to meet the condition requirements option for When to Run the Flow for Updated
Records.

Condition Requirements

| All Conditions Are Met (AND) ▼ |

Field	Operator	Value	
Status	Equals ▼	Closed - Not Converted	🗑

+ Add Condition

When to Run the Flow for Updated Records ❶

◉ Every time a record is updated and meets the condition requirements
○ Only when a record is updated to meet the condition requirements

* Optimize the Flow for:

Fast Field Updates	**Actions and Related Records** ✓
Update fields on the record that triggers the flow to run. This high-performance flow runs *before* the record is saved to the database.	Update any record and perform actions, like send an email. This more flexible flow runs *after* the record is saved to the database.

☐ Include a Run Asynchronously path to access an external system after the original transaction for the triggering record is successfully committed

Figure 6-13. *Configuring a Record-triggered flow*

5. Pamela navigates to the `Flow Designer`, clicks the `plus` icon, and selects the `Delete Records` element. This opens a new window, where she enters the following details.

   a. **Label**: Pamela enters the label for the input currency field: **Delete lead records**.

   b. **API Name**: This field autopopulates based on the label.

   c. **Description**: Pamela writes some meaningful text so other developers and administrators can easily understand why this `Delete Records` element was created. When users select the `Delete Records` element in the `Explorer` tab, the description appears in the Description area.

   d. **How to Find Records to Delete**: Pamela selects the "Use the IDs stored in a record variable" or record collection variable option.

   e. **Delete Records of This Object Type**: She selects the object for which she wants to delete the record. In this case, she selects the `{!$Record}`object.

The `Delete Records` element looks like Figure 6-14.

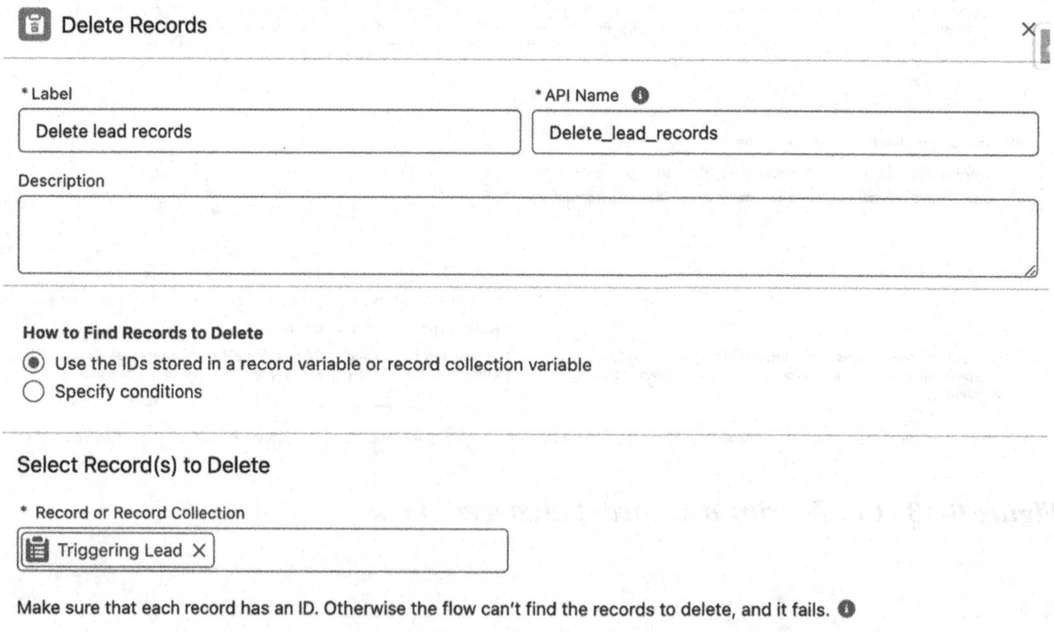

Figure 6-14. Configuring a `Delete Records` element

6. When she is finished, Pamela clicks the Done button.

7. Pamela clicks the Save button and enters **Delete unqualified leads** as the name by which to save the flow.

8. She activates the flow by clicking the Activate button.

Tip   To learn more about Salesforce Flow, refer to the Trailhead module at https://trailhead.salesforce.com/en/content/learn/modules/ business_process_automation.

The next time a user updates a lead to unqualified, the process Pamela created (using Process Builder) will fire and delete the record.

Use Case 3: Update Child Records

Pamela receives another request from her manager: when an opportunity is updated as Closed Lost, update all related quotes to Denied.

There are several ways to handle this task.

- Use an Apex trigger.

- Use a Record-triggered flow.

- Use a combination of Salesforce Flow and Inline Visualforce Page on the Opportunity detail page.

Pamela decides to use Record-triggered flow because it is fast and doesn't require coding skills. She performs the following steps.

1. She navigates to Setup (gear icon) ➤ Setup ➤ Process Automation ➤ Flow.

2. She clicks the New Flow button, which opens a pop-up, where she selects the Record-Triggered Flow option, and then clicks the Create button, which opens Salesforce Flow.

    a. Select the Record-Triggered Flow option, click Create, and configure the flow as follows.

    b. Object: Opportunity

c. Trigger the Flow When: A record is updated

d. Set Entry Criteria

e. Condition Requirements: StageName = Closed Lost

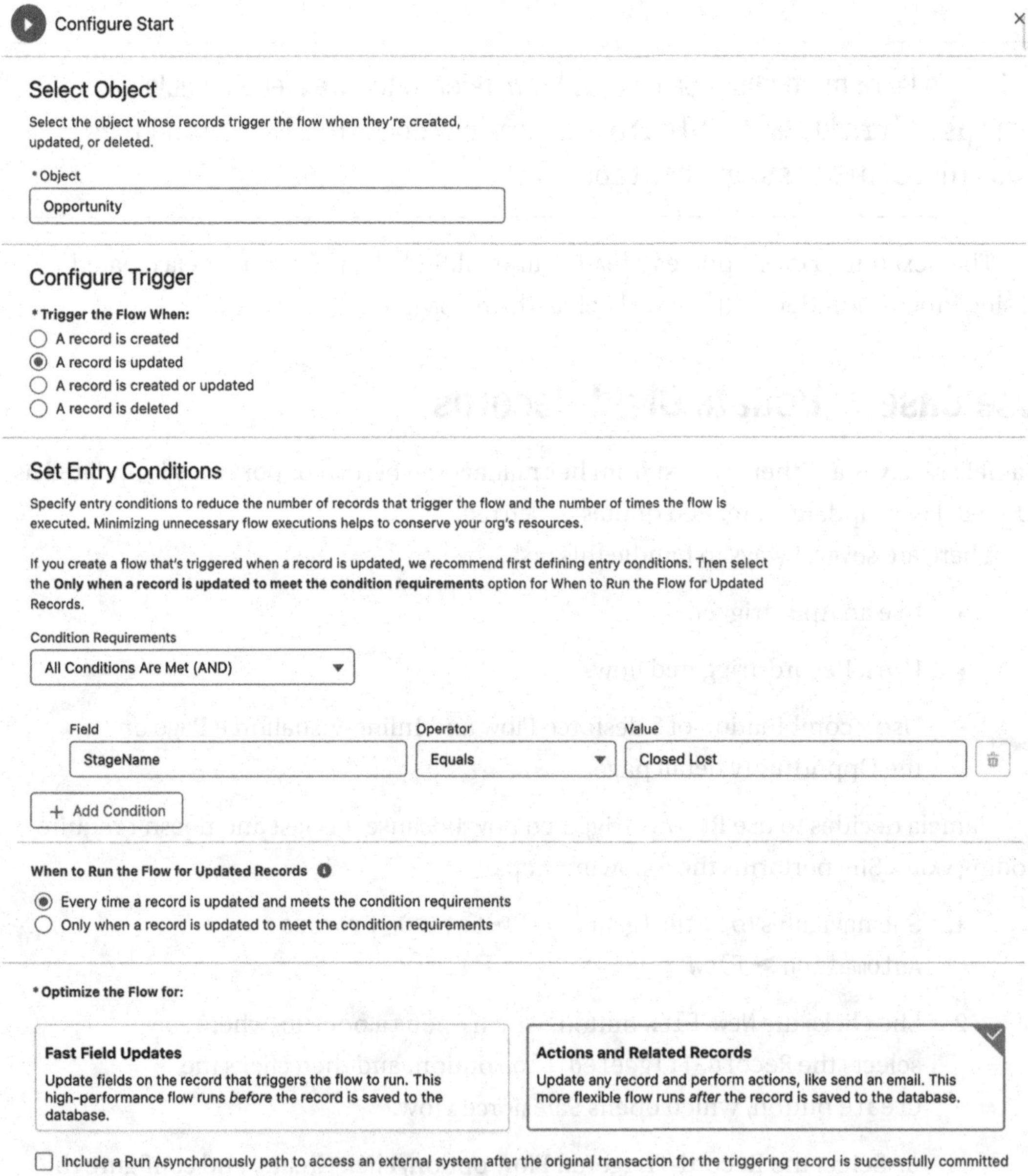

▶ Configure Start   ✕

Select Object

Select the object whose records trigger the flow when they're created,
updated, or deleted.

* Object

Opportunity

Configure Trigger

* Trigger the Flow When:

○ A record is created
◉ A record is updated
○ A record is created or updated
○ A record is deleted

Set Entry Conditions

Specify entry conditions to reduce the number of records that trigger the flow and the number of times the flow is
executed. Minimizing unnecessary flow executions helps to conserve your org's resources.

If you create a flow that's triggered when a record is updated, we recommend first defining entry conditions. Then select
the **Only when a record is updated to meet the condition requirements** option for When to Run the Flow for Updated
Records.

Condition Requirements

All Conditions Are Met (AND)   ▼

Field	Operator	Value	
StageName	Equals ▼	Closed Lost	🗑

┌ + Add Condition ┐

When to Run the Flow for Updated Records ℹ

◉ Every time a record is updated and meets the condition requirements
○ Only when a record is updated to meet the condition requirements

---

* Optimize the Flow for:

Fast Field Updates	**Actions and Related Records**
Update fields on the record that triggers the flow to run. This high-performance flow runs *before* the record is saved to the database.	Update any record and perform actions, like send an email. This more flexible flow runs *after* the record is saved to the database.

☐ Include a Run Asynchronously path to access an external system after the original transaction for the triggering record is successfully committed

Figure 6-15. *Configuring a Record-triggered flow*

3. Pamela navigates to the Flow Designer, clicks the plus icon, and selects the Update Records element. This opens a new window, where she enters the following details.

   a. **Label**: She enters the label for the input currency field: **Related Quotes = Denied**.

   b. **API Name**: This field autopopulates based on the label.

   c. **Description**: Pamela writes some meaningful text so other developers and administrators can easily understand why this Delete Records element was created. When users select the Delete Records element in the Explorer tab, the description appears in the Description area.

   d. **How to Find Records to Update and Set Their Values**: Pamela selects the "Update records related to the opportunity record that triggered the flow" option.

   e. **Records Related to Opportunity**: She selects the {!$Record.Quotes} object to update the status.

   f. **Set Field Values for the Quote Records:** Pamela selects Status in the Field option and Denied in the Value option.

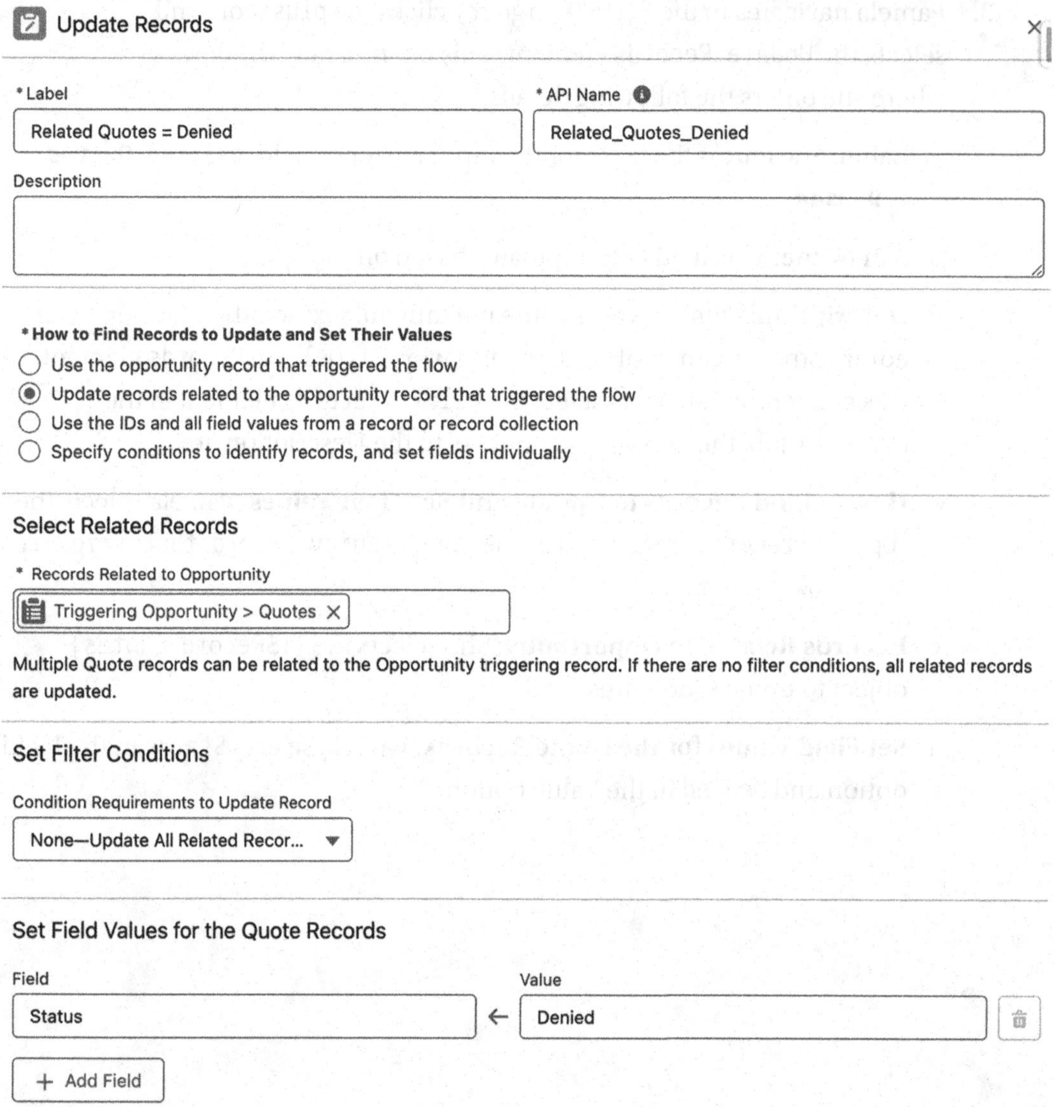

Update Records   ✕

*Label	*API Name ⓘ
Related Quotes = Denied	Related_Quotes_Denied

Description

*How to Find Records to Update and Set Their Values

○ Use the opportunity record that triggered the flow
◉ Update records related to the opportunity record that triggered the flow
○ Use the IDs and all field values from a record or record collection
○ Specify conditions to identify records, and set fields individually

Select Related Records

* Records Related to Opportunity

📋 Triggering Opportunity > Quotes ✕

Multiple Quote records can be related to the Opportunity triggering record. If there are no filter conditions, all related records are updated.

Set Filter Conditions

Condition Requirements to Update Record

None—Update All Related Recor... ▼

Set Field Values for the Quote Records

Field		Value	
Status	←	Denied	🗑

+ Add Field

Figure 6-16. *Configuring a Record Records element*

4. When she is finished, Pamela clicks the Done button.

5. Pamela clicks the Save button and enters **Update Quotes = Denied** as the name by which to save the flow.

6. She activates the flow by clicking the Activate button.

The next time a user updates an opportunity to Closed Lost, the process Pamela created (using Process Builder) fires and sets quotes to Denied.

Tip   To learn about when to use before-save vs. after-save flows, read the article at `https://automationchampion.com/2020/12/15/when-to-use-before-save-vs-after-save-record-triggered-flows/`.

Introduction to Approval Processes

Almost every organization uses some sort of approval process. For example, if you want to take a day or two off, you may need to get approval from your manager to do so. An approval process is a way an organization approves anything from invoices, budgets, and purchase orders to a new process the company wants to incorporate. Implementing an approval process can standardize an organization's internal processes, which saves time by creating a dependable, repeatable process. Approval processes are a type of workflow, which is any sequence of work from initiation to completion, that you can create to ensure work is approved the same way every time.

The approval process in Salesforce is an automated process used to approve records in Salesforce. You can specify what happens when records are approved or rejected by the approver.

Wizards to Create an Approval Process

Salesforce offers two types of wizards to create approval processes.

- **Jump Start Wizard**: Use this wizard to create a one-step approval process. This wizard allows you to create an approval process quickly. Everything is available on the same screen, so a user does not have to navigate through several screens.

- **Standard Wizard**: Use this wizard to create multistep approval processes. This wizard consists of setup wizards that allow users to define a process and another setup wizard that allows users to define each step in the process.

Once again, Pamela has received a new request: create an approval process on the Opportunity object. Approval must be requested from the company's CEO (Rakesh Gupta) if the opportunity amount is greater than US$5,000,000.

Pamela decides to use the standard wizard to create the approval process on the Opportunity object. Before proceeding, she makes sure she has the Approval Status picklist on the Opportunity object, as shown in Table 6-1.

Table 6-1. *Create a Custom Field*

Field Type	Label	Length/Values
Picklist	Status	Submitted
		Approved
		Rejected

Creating a New Approval Process

Pamela performs the following steps in Salesforce Experience to create a new approval process on the Opportunity object.

1. She navigates to Setup (gear icon) ➤ All Setup ➤ PLATFORM TOOLS ➤ Process Automation ➤ Approval Processes.

2. From the Manage Approval Processes For drop-down, she selects the Opportunity object.

3. Next, she selects "Create new approval process" from the drop-down menu and then selects Use Standard Setup Wizard.

4. She enters the following information.

    a. **Process Name**: Pamela types **$5M deal approval process**.

    b. **Unique Name**: This field is autopopulated based on the process name.

    c. **Description**: Pamela enters a meaningful description of the approval process so other administrators can understand easily why this approval process was created.

5. When done, she clicks the Next button.

6. Pamela specifies the entry criteria. When done, her screen looks like Figure 6-17.

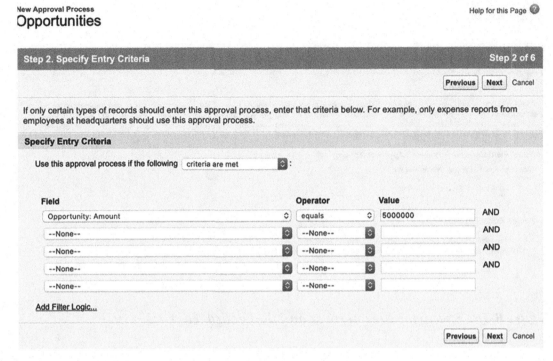

Figure 6-17. *Specifying entry criteria*

When done, she clicks the Next button.

7. Pamela defines the following actions.

a. **Select Field Used for Automated Approval Routing**: The approval process allows an approval process creator to assign approval requests to any user. Another option is to use a user field to route approval requests automatically. The user field can be any custom hierarchical relationship field, such as Reporting Manager or the manager standard user field. Pamela leaves this as is.

b. **Record Editability Properties**: When a record is submitted for approval, it gets locked. The process allows Pamela to define who can edit the record during an approval process. She selects the "Administrators OR the currently assigned approver can edit records during the approval process" option.

Pamela's screen looks like Figure 6-18.

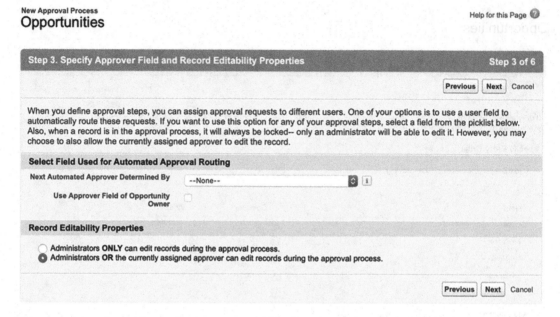

Figure 6-18. Specifying the approver and the Record Editability Properties field

When done, she clicks the Next button.

8. When an approval process assigns an approval request to a user, it automatically sends an email notification to the user. The email contains a link to the approval page. If you want to use your custom email template, then choose a template or leave it blank. If you leave it blank, Salesforce uses the default email template. When done, Pamela clicks the Next button.

9. On the Select Fields to Display on Approval Page Layout screen, Pamela does the following.

    a. She selects the fields she wants to display on the Approval Request page.

    b. She selects the "Display approval history information in addition to the fields selected above." check box to display the approval history-related list on the Approval Request page.

    c. In the Security Settings section, Pamela selects where users can approve or reject a request. She selects the "Allow approvers to access the approval page from within the salesforce.com application or externally from a wireless-enabled mobile device" option.

Her screen looks like Figure 6-19.

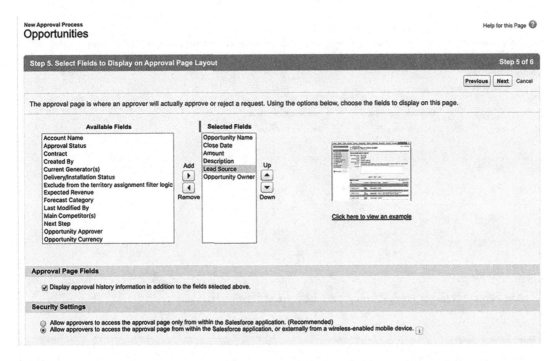

Figure 6-19. *Selecting fields to display on the Approval Request page*

When done, Pamela clicks the Next button.

10.   Pamela specifies the initial submitters (see Figure 6-20). She does
this as follows.

a. In the Submitter Type section, she selects Opportunity Owner.

b. She selects the "Add the Approval History related list to all
Registration page layouts" check box to add the approval history-
related list to the Account page.

c. Pamela selects the "Allow submitters to recall approval requests"
check box. This allows the submitter to recall the approval process.

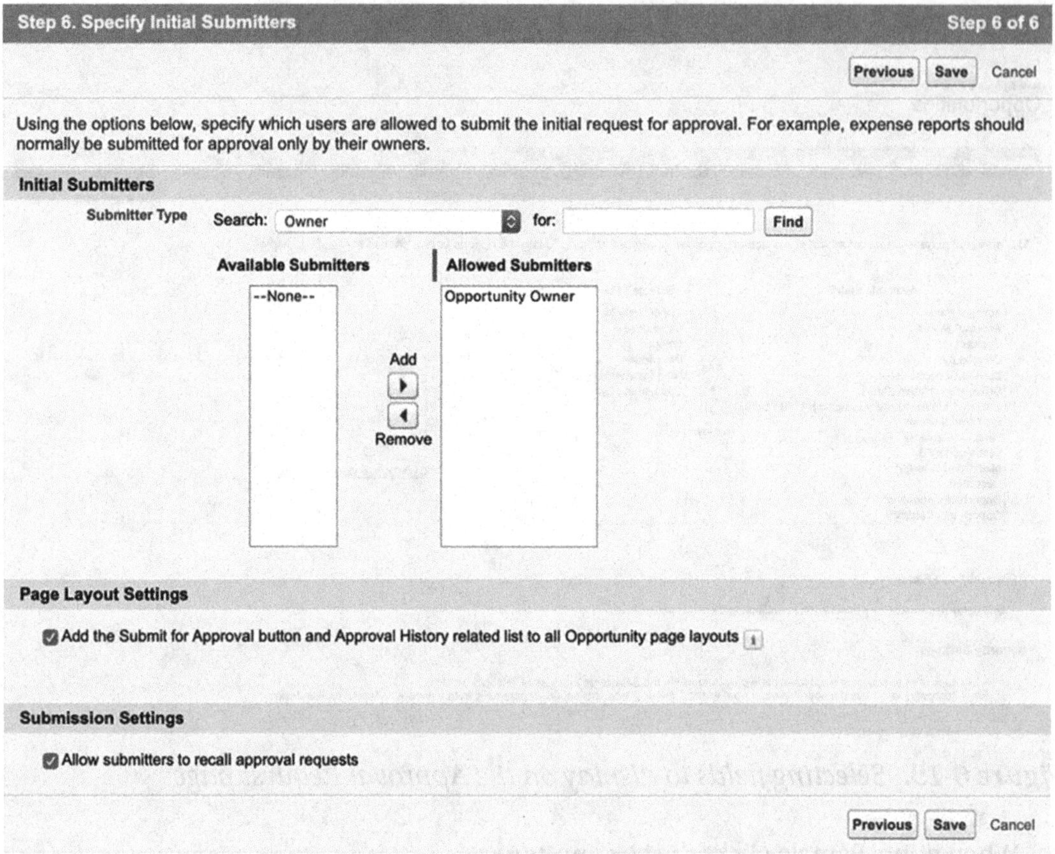

Figure 6-20. *Specifying initial submitters*

11. When done, she clicks the Save button. In the next screen, she
    selects the "No, I'll do this later. Take me back to the
    listing of all approval processes for this object"
    option. The system redirects her to the screen shown in
    Figure 6-21.

Process Definition Detail   [Edit ▾] [Clone] [Delete] [Activate]

Process Name	$5M deal approval Process	Active	☐
Unique Name	X5M_deal_approval_Process	Next Automated Approver Determined By	
Description			
Entry Criteria	Opportunity: Amount EQUALS "USD 5,000,000"		
Record Editability	Administrator **OR** Current Approver	Allow Submitters to Recall Approval Requests	✓
Approval Assignment Email Template			
Approval Post Template			
Initial Submitters	Opportunity Owner		
Created By	Rakesh Gupta, 9/8/2019 1:37 PM	Modified By	Rakesh Gupta, 10/3/2019 4:51 PM

Initial Submission Actions ⓘ   [Add Existing] [Add New ▾]

Action	Type	Description
	Record Lock	Lock the record from being edited
Edit | Remove	Field Update	Approval status = Submitted

Approval Steps ⓘ   [New Approval Step]

Action	Step Number	Name	Description	Criteria	Assigned Approver	Reject Behavior
Show Actions | Edit | Del	1	Approval from CEO			User:Rakesh Gupta	Final Rejection

Final Approval Actions ⓘ   [Add Existing] [Add New ▾]

Action	Type	Description
Edit	Record Lock	Unlock the record for editing

Final Rejection Actions ⓘ   [Add Existing] [Add New ▾]

Action	Type	Description
Edit	Record Lock	Unlock the record for editing

Recall Actions ⓘ   [Add Existing] [Add New ▾]

Action	Type	Description
	Record Lock	Unlock the record for editing

Figure 6-21. *Approval process detail page*

Final Approval Actions

Final approval happens only when a record has received all the required approvals. For the current scenario, Pamela navigates to the Final Approval Actions section, then clicks the Edit link and selects the "Unlock the record for editing" option, as shown in Figure 6-22.

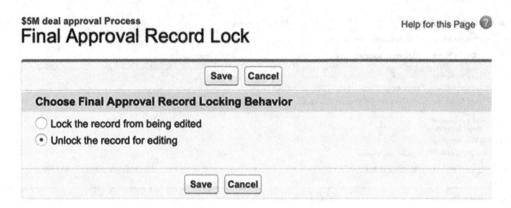

Figure 6-22. *Final approval action*

When done, she clicks the Save button. She repeats these steps for the Final Rejection and Recall actions.

Initial Submission Actions

The initial action happens only when a record is initially submitted for approval. When the record is submitted successfully for approval, it gets locked. You can define actions such as Field Update, Email Alert, Assign Task, and Outbound Message. Add one initial submission action to update the Approval Status field to Submitted, as shown in Figure 6-23.

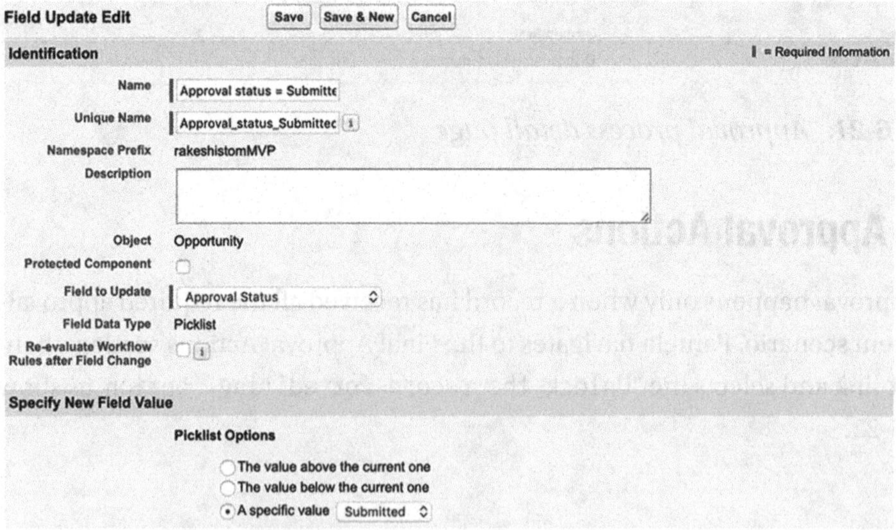

Figure 6-23. *Initial submission action*

This field update executes when an Opportunity record is submitted for the CEO's approval.

Approval Steps

Pamela needs to add approval steps. The first step is to get approval from the CEO (Rakesh Gupta). Pamela performs the following actions to achieve this.

1. She navigates to the Approval Steps section and then clicks the New Approval Step button.

2. Next, she enters the following details.

    a. **Name**: Pamela types **Approval from CEO**.

    b. **Unique Name**: The unique name is autopopulated based on the name.

    c. **Description**: Pamela enters a meaningful description of the approval step so other developers and administrators can easily understand why this second approval step has been created.

    d. When done, she clicks the Next button.

3. Now Pamela needs to filter out records. She decides which record should enter the approval step. She can filter out a record by adding more conditions. For example, suppose she wants to filter the Opportunity record that is referred by partners. For this scenario, she would select All records should enter this step, then click the Next button.

4. In the next screen, Pamela selects User ➤ Rakesh Gupta. Her screen now looks like Figure 6-24.

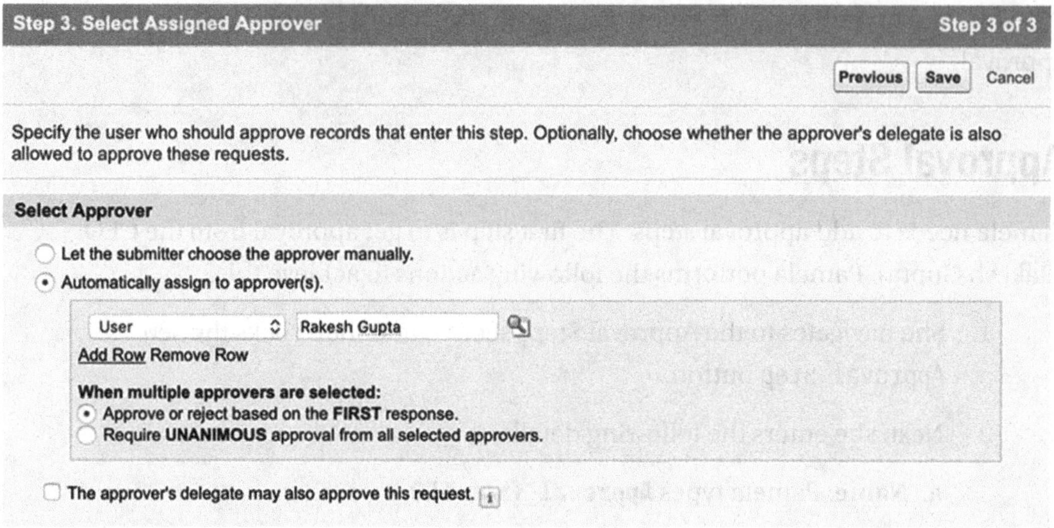

Step 3. Select Assigned Approver   Step 3 of 3

Previous   Save   Cancel

Specify the user who should approve records that enter this step. Optionally, choose whether the approver's delegate is also allowed to approve these requests.

Select Approver

○ Let the submitter choose the approver manually.
◉ Automatically assign to approver(s).

| User ⌄ | Rakesh Gupta | 🔍 |

Add Row Remove Row

When multiple approvers are selected:
◉ Approve or reject based on the **FIRST** response.
○ Require **UNANIMOUS** approval from all selected approvers.

☐ The approver's delegate may also approve this request. ⓘ

Figure 6-24. *Selecting an assigned approver*

5. When done, she clicks the Save button.

6. On the next screen, Pamela selects the "No, I'll do this later. Take me to the approval process detail page to review what I've just created" option. She is then redirected to the approval process detail page.

7. She adds field updates to the Approval Actions and Rejection Actions sections to update the Status field to Approved or Rejected, as shown in Figure 6-25.

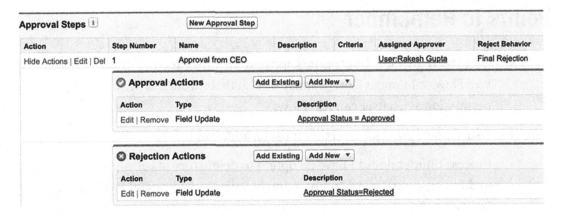

Figure 6-25. *Field updates to show* Approval *or* Rejection *actions*

Pamela has now created a multistep approval process. She can view the approval process diagram by clicking View Diagram.

Activating an Approval Process

Pamela knows she must activate the approval process by clicking the Activate button at the top of the approval process page, as shown in Figure 6-26.

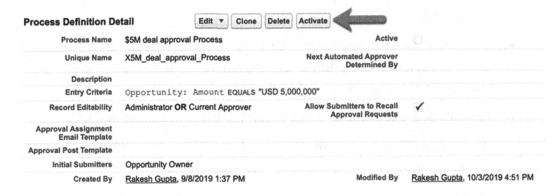

Figure 6-26. *Activating an approval process*

Before activating it, however, she makes sure no more changes are required because once an approval process is active, it is not possible to add more steps to it.

Points to Remember

- Users with the Flow User permissions on their user record. And, Run Flow or Manage Flow permissions on their profile, or via a permission set, a user can run Flow.

- To activate a process, an action must be added to it.

- Process Builder doesn't have an option to delete records. If you want to do so, you must use a combination of Salesforce Flow and Process Builder.

- The process/flow owner, or last modified user, receives an email from Salesforce if the process fails during runtime or if any other fault occurs. Use the Apex Exception Email option to distribute such errors to other users.

- A process has the same governing limits as that of Apex.

- Process actions are executed in the same order in which they appear in the process.

- You can't delete an active process. If you want to do so, you must first deactivate it.

- If you leave the Next Automated Approver Determined By field blank, you can't assign approval requests automatically to the manager in any step you create for an approval process.

- You can use Process Builder to autosubmit the record for approval.

- Use the Mass Transfer Approval Requests wizard to "mass transfer" pending approval requests from one user to another user.

- You can create and run approval history reports to check in-progress and completed approval processes and their steps.

Hands-on Exercises

The following exercises give you more practice with the platform, which ultimately will help you gain mastery of it and assist you in preparing for the certification examination. Remember, these are hands-on exercises, and you can find the answers in the appendix, but try to implement them in your Salesforce org, which is the primary goal of doing them. Try to do the exercises without looking at the answers!

1. Create a flow that displays three number fields: First Number, Second Number, and Third Number. On the next screen, show the summation of the values in these fields.

2. Dennis Williams, a system administrator at GoC, receives a request to send a welcome email to new customers (contacts) as soon as a user is created in Salesforce. How would you instruct him to meet this requirement?

3. Dennis needs to keep the contact's phone number in sync with the account's Phone Number field. This means that whenever someone updates a phone number on an account, it should be reflected in the contact's record. How would you instruct him to fulfill this request?

4. Dennis wants to implement opportunity management at GoC, but he is a bit confused by one of the tasks. Because you now have a better understanding of process automation, please help him automate the business process for the following requirements.

   a. When an opportunity amount is greater than $1,000,000, create a post on the chatter group Key Deals.

   b. Whenever an opportunity is marked Closed Won, autoupdate the account description to "We won another deal!".

   c. Whenever an opportunity is marked Closed Won, notify the opportunity team on Salesforce mobile and in Salesforce Experience.

5. Dennis receives a requirement to add the permission set View All Leads automatically to new users. How would you instruct him to meet this request?

Summary

This chapter covered Salesforce Flow and Salesforce Flow Designer and its life cycle. It also went through different use cases of Salesforce Flow, reviewed Salesforce Process Builder via a few examples, and studied approval processes and how to configure them by looking at an example.

Chapter 7 examines the application development life cycle. So, stay tuned!

The Nuts and Bolts of Application Development

Abstract

Chapter 6 covered Lightning Flow, overviewed Lightning Process Builder, and examined approval processes using real-life examples.

This chapter looks at the limits of declarative customization and when to use programmatic development, examines the application development life cycle, including different types of sandboxes and deployment tools, and studies different deployment tools.

The Limits of Declarative Development

As awesome as out-of-the-box point-and-click features are, there are limits to their reach. For example, you've explored formula fields, validation rules, Process Builder, page layouts, and so on. These point-and-click tools make Salesforce even better, allowing for easy configuration and maintenance. The problem arises when you have a task that cannot be solved using out-of-the-box features.

Business Use Case 1

Pamela Kline is still working as a Salesforce administrator at GoC. She has discovered that sales reps are deleting Closed Lost opportunities, which is detrimental to accurate analytics, to say the least! Pamela wants to make sure that sales reps are only allowed to delete those opportunities that are not Closed Won or Closed Lost.

183

R. Gupta, *Salesforce Platform App Builder Certification Companion*, Certification Study Companion Series

How should Pamela meet this business requirement? If your answer is to use a validation rule, take a few minutes to ask yourself: when would the validation rule fire?

A validation rule fires only when a record is created or edited, not when a record is deleted. So now you know that using a validation rule is not the right thing to do. This use case also reveals the limitations of declarative solutions and indicates that you need to go beyond point-and-clicks toward code.

Solution: Use an Apex Trigger

There are several ways to meet Pamela's new business requirement, but the best way to do so is to write an Apex trigger on the Opportunity object as follows.

```
trigger opportunityValidation(before delete){
    for(Opportunity opp: Trigger.new){
        if(opp.StageName == 'Closed Won' || opp.StageName == 'Closed Lost'){
            Opp.AddError(You are not allowed to delete closed won or closed
            lost opportunity);
        }
    }
}
```

A trigger is executed during Data Manipulation Language (DML) database actions. For example, you can create a trigger on the Account object that executes whenever an Account record is updated or deleted. Therefore, triggers are called implicitly from a database action.

Business Use Case 2

Pamela Kline just received another task from her manager: whenever a new account is approved in Salesforce, create a PDF that is sent to all contacts on that account.

Let's take a few minutes to pause and think. Can you use a point-and-click solution here? If your answer is no, then you are on the right track!

Solution 1: Use a Visualforce Page

There are various solutions available in the market to generate PDF documents from Salesforce, but one thing they all have in common is that they are built using custom development.

To meet the request, Pamela (or her developer) can create a simple Visualforce page as follows.

```
<apex:page showHeader="false" standardController="Account"
standardStylesheets="false" renderAs="PDF">
//Your logic goes here
</apex:page>
```

Visualforce is a framework that includes a tag-based markup language. It allows you to build sophisticated, attractive, and dynamic custom user interfaces. You can use almost all standard web technologies—such as CSS, jQuery, and HTML5—with a Visualforce page. This means you can build a rich user interface for any device, including mobile, tablet, and so on.

Solution 2: Use an AppExchange App

An alternative solution for Pamela is to use Salesforce AppExchange apps such as Conga, Drawloop, Nintex, DocGen, and so on.

Are you wondering whether it is better to write Apex code or use apps from an AppExchange app? The answer should always depend on the availability of time, budget, and ability to meet expectations.

The pros and cons of using Apex vs. leveraging AppExchange are as follows: custom development offers flexibility and a highly tailored solution to meet your specific needs and expectations in a highly granular manner. However, precisely because of this, it may take longer to build and, as a result, may cost more. AppExchange apps, on the other hand, may not meet all your needs completely, but the apps will be up and running in hours if not minutes. As a result, the end product may be cheaper. In such a situation, the best practice is to do a gap analysis and, based on the outcome, opt for one or the other solution.

Business Use Case 3

Pamela's manager wants to provide detailed information about GoC's potential customers, such as the weather in the city where a contact resides, to sales reps. To achieve this, GoC wants to display weather information based on a contact's mailing city. What do you think? How should Pamela solve this need? Does Salesforce have any out-of-the-box functionality to achieve this?

Solution: Use APIs

Unfortunately, Salesforce doesn't have any out-of-the-box functionality to meet Pamela's new task. So, how should she handle it? The answer is to use an *application program interface* (API). Websites like Weather.com and AccuWeather offer APIs so that developers can get information. Using APIs, it is possible to get weather information based on a customer's mailing location.

Use Case Summary

As the three scenarios discussed in this section demonstrate, the best practice is to assess the pros and cons of declarative customization vs. programmatic development. When you start working on real projects or with a Trailhead module (which I strongly suggest), you will master the art of deciding the best path forward—be it declarative, programmatic, or both!

Managing the Application Life Cycle

Application life cycle management entails end-to-end management of the software development process. The process includes governance, development, and operation. The software development life cycle (also known as SDLC), on the other hand, focuses primarily on the development phase.

Depending on your software development methodology (waterfall, Agile, or DevOps), application life cycle management might be split into separate phases or may be fully integrated into a continuous delivery process. Regardless, application life cycle management can be broken down into three categories: governance, development, and operations.

Application Governance

Application governance teams start by gathering requirements from business stakeholders. Architects or solution designers create design documentation. The team then hands over the document to a development team for implementation.

Application Development

Next comes the development stage of application life cycle management. SDLC includes building, testing, releasing the build, releasing the test, and updating the application.

Application Operations

The third step in application life cycle management is operations. Operations include the deployment of the application and maintenance of the technology (which is not applicable in Salesforce).

Sandboxes

No sandbox comes with a developer org. Fortunately, Salesforce's free developer edition org is used to perform the tasks and exercises in this book. Because developer orgs are yours forever, you can keep practicing in such orgs even if you switch jobs.

This, however, is not the same when you work on your company's org. You lose access to the org when you switch jobs. The advantage of being on a company's Salesforce org is that you get access to at least one sandbox org. A sandbox is like a developer org except that it is affiliated with a company's production org. A sandbox allows you to build and test business processes in a controlled environment without negatively impacting your production org. When you know your workflow rules, formula fields, and flows are working correctly in a sandbox, you can migrate them to your production org. You can create a sandbox from production or a live org.

Why do you need a sandbox when you have a free developer org? A free developer org comes with a few limitations, including the following.

- Data storage: 5 MB

- File storage: 20 MB

- Salesforce licenses: 2

- A fewer number of API calls per day

When you start working on a real project, you may need a playground that allows you to work with more data and file storage, including more API calls per day and more Salesforce licenses, so you can create more than two user accounts if required.

There are different types of sandboxes, as summarized in Table 7-1.

Table 7-1. *Sandbox Types and Their Differences*

Sandbox Type	Refresh Interval	Storage Limit	Sandbox Template	What Copied
Developer	1 day	Data storage: 200 MB File storage: 200 MB	No	Metadata only
Developer Pro	1 day	Data storage: 1 GB File storage: 1 GB	No	Metadata only
Partial copy	5 days	Data storage: 5 GB File storage: 5 GB	Required	Metadata and sample data
Full	29 days	The same as your production org	Available	Metadata and all data (or sample data, if a sandbox template is being used), and chatter and history (optional)

In Table 7-1, *metadata* means all configurations, Apex code, and all users. The refresh interval is often referred to when discussing sandboxes. To *refresh* a sandbox means to copy fresh information from other sandboxes or a production org.

Let's look at the different types of available sandboxes more closely to help you choose the sandbox you would use for a project.

Developer Sandbox

Use a developer sandbox for isolated development purposes. In general, each organization has a good volume of such sandboxes. If you have seven developers working on a project, you can create seven developer sandboxes and give a separate sandbox to each developer. This eliminates the possibility of developers overwriting others' work. This sandbox includes your production org's metadata (Apex, all users, and other configurations). A developer sandbox can be refreshed once a day.

Developer Pro Sandbox

Like the developer sandbox, the dev pro sandbox is used for development, Apex testing, and unit testing. A dev pro sandbox has a higher storage limit compared to a developer sandbox. Higher limits allow developers to test an application with larger datasets. Like a developer sandbox, a dev pro sandbox also includes your production org's metadata (Apex, all users, and configurations). It can be refreshed once a day, too.

Partial Sandbox

A partial sandbox contains a subset of data from your production org. The specific subset of data you include in the partial sandbox is defined in a sandbox template. A partial sandbox can be used for user acceptance testing, regression testing, and so forth. Unlike a developer sandbox and a dev pro sandbox, a partial sandbox can only be refreshed every five days.

Full Sandbox

A full sandbox is a replica of your production org. It can contain metadata such as attachments, object records, and users. In addition, it can also include chatter and field history data. This type of sandbox is used for integration testing, staging, and production debugging. It can be refreshed every 29 days.

Setting up a Sandbox

Let's rejoin Pamela Kline, who understands the importance of sandboxes. She wants to set up a developer sandbox so she can do configuration there. Pamela performs the following steps to create a developer sandbox.

1. She navigates to Setup (gear icon) ➤ Setup ➤ Environments ➤ Sandboxes.

2. Next, Pamela clicks New Sandbox, as shown in Figure 7-1.

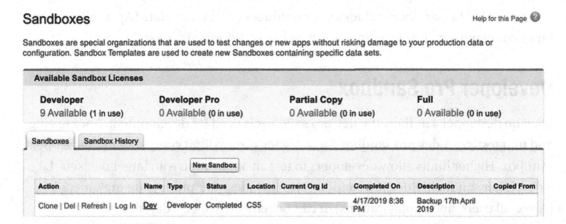

Figure 7-1. *Creating a new sandbox*

3. Pamela enters the sandbox name Dev1 and, from the Create From drop-down, she selects Production, as shown in Figure 7-2.

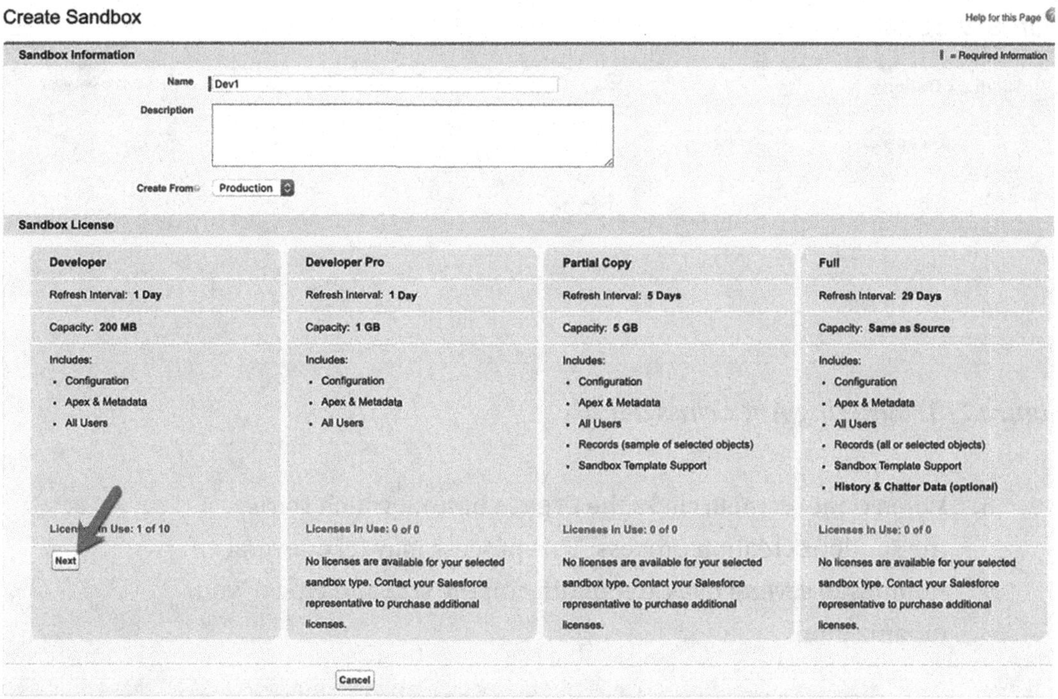

Figure 7-2. *Entering sandbox details*

4.   Pamela clicks the Next button available in the Developer section.
The system redirects Pamela to a new window to specify the Apex
class she created previously from the SandboxPostCopy interface,
which runs the scripts after each create and refresh for this
sandbox. In this scenario, Pamela leaves this field blank, as shown
in Figure 7-3.

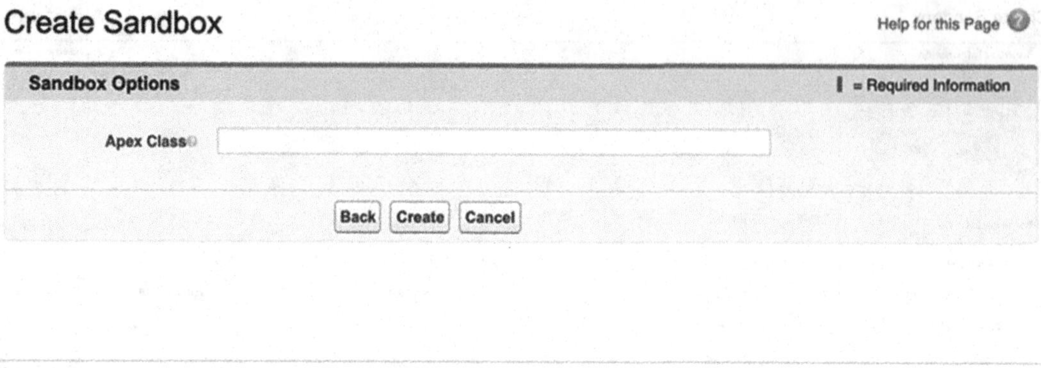

Create Sandbox

Sandbox Options		= Required Information
Apex Class		

Back   Create   Cancel

Figure 7-3. *Entering Apex class details*

5. When done, Pamela clicks the Create button, which starts the sandbox creation process. This process may take several minutes to several days, depending on the size and type of your organization.

Accessing a Sandbox

You've seen how to set up a sandbox, but how do you access it? If you recall, the setup process didn't ask us to set up a user account for our new sandbox!

Let's rejoin Pamela. She performs the following steps to access her newly created sandbox.

1. When the sandbox is ready, Pamela receives an email from Salesforce asking her to activate it, which she does.

2. The username is the production username appended by the sandbox name. For example, Pamela's production username is pamela@goc.com, and the sandbox name is Dev1. As a result, the sandbox username is pamela@goc.com.dev1.

3. The password is the same as the production password.

Deployment

Pamela works in her newly created sandbox environment, which is the best way to configure or customize applications in Salesforce. She wants to understand how to move metadata from her sandbox to the production org.

When you create a field or metadata in a sandbox, it is not automatically available in the production org. To deploy the metadata between Salesforce environments, Pamela must use one of the following options.

- Change sets

- Packages

- Integrated development environments (IDEs, such as SFDX or Force.com)

- Force.com migration tool

- Third-party deployment tools (such as Copado)

Deploy Using Change Sets

Change sets are the easiest way to deploy metadata between *connected* orgs. For example, you can use change sets to deploy a metadata component from sandbox to production, sandbox to sandbox, and production to sandbox.

Change sets include containers that hold metadata components. They can only be used to deploy *metadata components*, not data or records. To use change sets, make sure both organizations have a deployment connection setup. There are two types of change sets: outbound and inbound.

Outbound Change Sets

Outbound change sets can be used to send metadata components from a sandbox to production or another sandbox.

Pamela, our hardworking system administrator, has created the custom field `Anniversary Date` on the `Contact` object in a sandbox. Now, she wants to migrate the field to the production org. She performs the following steps to create an outbound change set.

1. Pamela logs in to the sandbox environment at `https://test.salesforce.com`.

2. She navigates to Setup (gear icon) ➤ `Setup Home` ➤ `PLATFORM TOOLS` ➤ `Environments` ➤ `Change Sets` ➤ `Outbound Change Sets`.

3. In the Change Sets section, she clicks the `New` button to create a new outbound change set, as shown in Figure 7-4.

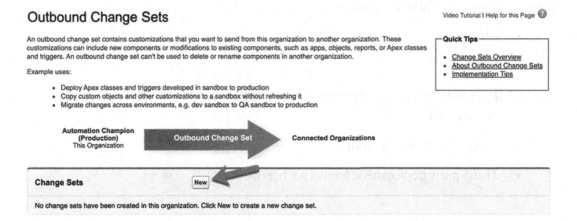

Figure 7-4. *Creating a new outbound change set*

4. This action opens a window, and Pamela enters the following details.

   - **Name:** She enters a meaningful name for the outbound change set: `Anniversary Date`.

   - **Description:** Pamela writes some meaningful text so other developers and administrators can easily understand why this outbound change set was created in the first place.

Her screen looks like Figure 7-5.

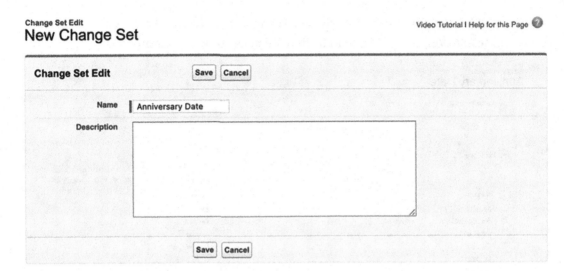

Figure 7-5. *Entering change set details*

5. When done, she clicks the Save button.

6. Next, Pamela must add all the metadata components she wants
    to deploy to the target org. To do so, she navigates to the Change
    Set Components section and clicks the Add button, as shown in
    Figure 7-6.

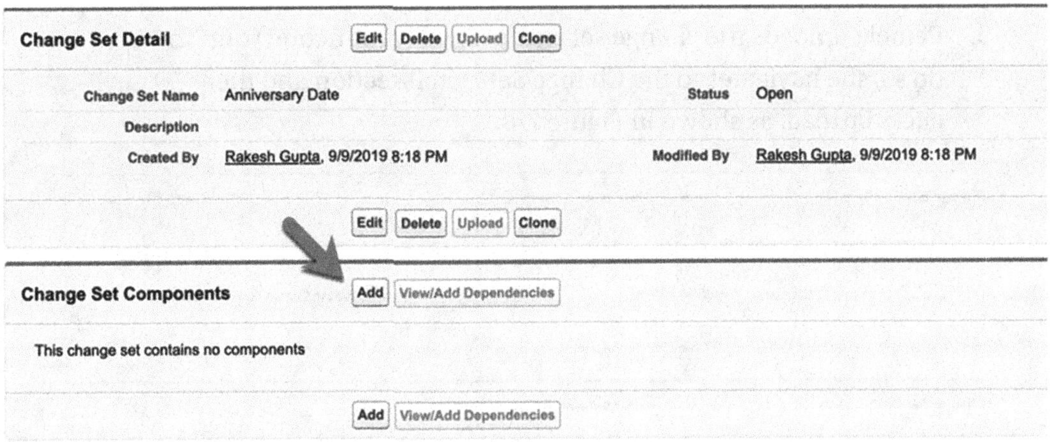

Figure 7-6. *Outbound change set components*

7. For Component Type, she selects Custom Field. Then, she selects the Anniversary Date field from the list, as shown in Figure 7-7.

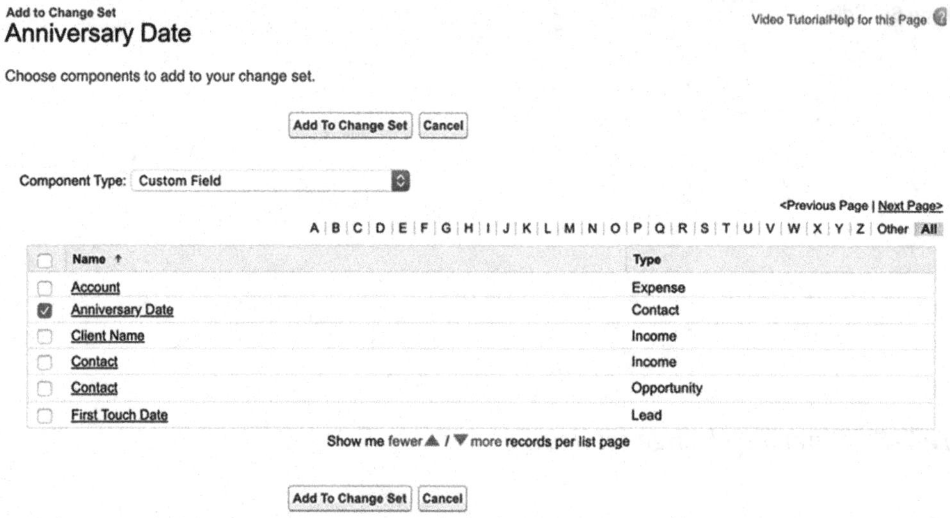

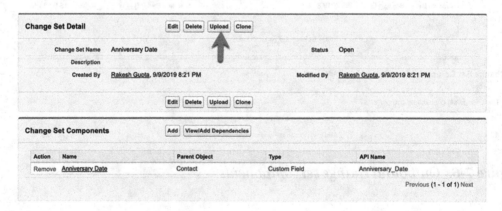

Figure 7-7. *Adding components to the change set*

8. When done, she clicks the Add To Change Set button. If Pamela had wanted to add multiple metadata components to her outbound change set, she would have repeated steps 6 and 7.

9. Pamela uploads the change set to the target (production) org. To do so, she navigates to the Change Set Detail section and then clicks Upload, as shown in Figure 7-8.

Figure 7-8. *Uploading a change set*

10. Pamela then selects the target organization from the Upload Details section and specifies where she wants to upload the change set. She selects Production, as shown in Figure 7-9.

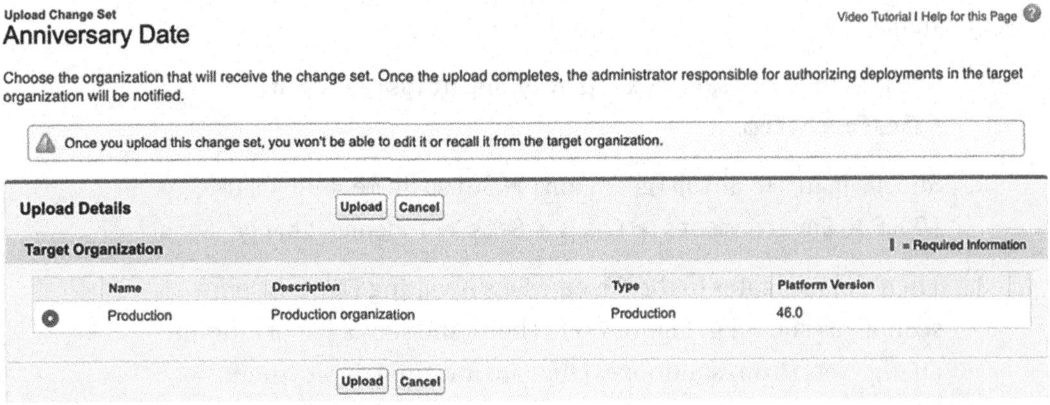

Figure 7-9. *Selecting a target org*

If, in the target org, inbound change set access was not granted for the current sandbox, Pamela wouldn't be able to select her target org from the list. In this case, she would have to return to the production org and enable it.

11. When done, Pamela clicks the Upload button. If the upload is successful, she'll see a message on-screen, as shown in Figure 7-10. She also receives an email from Salesforce, affirming her change set upload was successful.

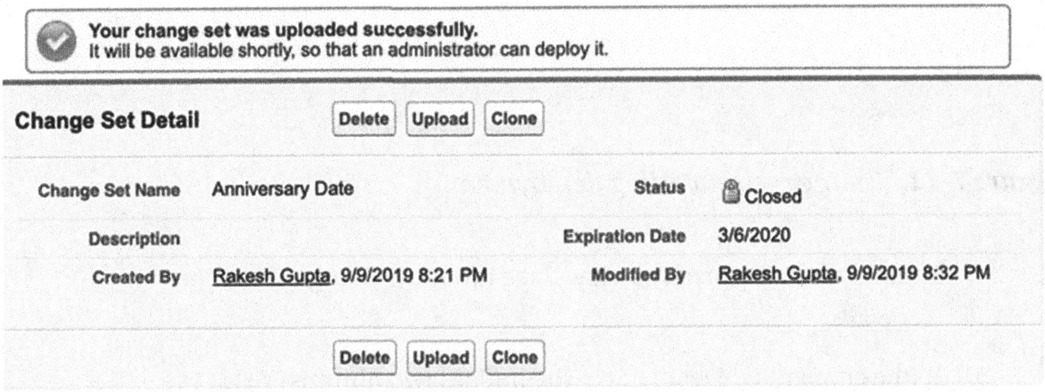

Figure 7-10. *Upload success message*

Inbound Change Sets

Inbound change sets can be used to receive metadata components from a sandbox to production or other sandboxes. Pamela performs the following steps to deploy an inbound change.

1. She logs in to her sandbox org by typing **https://login. salesforce.com**.

2. She navigates to Setup (gear icon) ➤ Setup Home ➤ PLATFORM TOOLS ➤ Environments ➤ Change Sets ➤ Inbound Change Sets.

3. Then she navigates to the Change Sets Awaiting Deployment section, as shown in Figure 7-11. There, she sees a list of inbound change sets (from sandboxes) that are awaiting deployment.

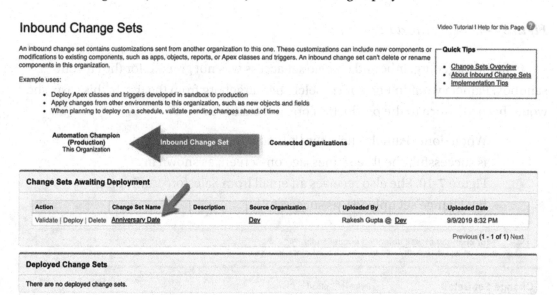

Figure 7-11. *Change sets awaiting deployment*

4. Pamela clicks the Anniversary Date inbound change set to view its details.

5. In the change sed Detail page, she notices two buttons: Validate and Deploy.

- **Validate**: Pamela knows she can use this button to simulate an actual deployment. She would be able to view the success or failure messages received with an actual deployment.

- **Deploy**: Pamela also knows that she uses the Deploy button to deploy the change set, which is done in a single operation. If the deployment is unable to complete (if it fails for any reason), the entire transaction is rolled back.

Pamela knows the best practice is to validate the change set first. When it's successful, she would then deploy it.

6. Pamela clicks Validate and notes that the simulated change set deployment is a success.

7. She then deploys the change set by clicking Deploy. Pamela could select a test class to run, but she defaults and clicks Deploy. A warning message states that once a change set is deployed, it cannot be rollbacked.

8. Pamela clicks the OK button and sees a message while the upload is in progress, as shown in Figure 7-12.

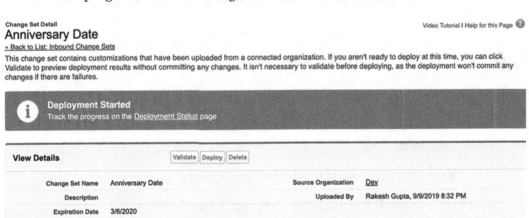

Figure 7-12. *Upload started*

9. When the upload is finished, whether a success or a failure, Pamela sees it listed in the Deployment History section, as shown in Figure 7-13.

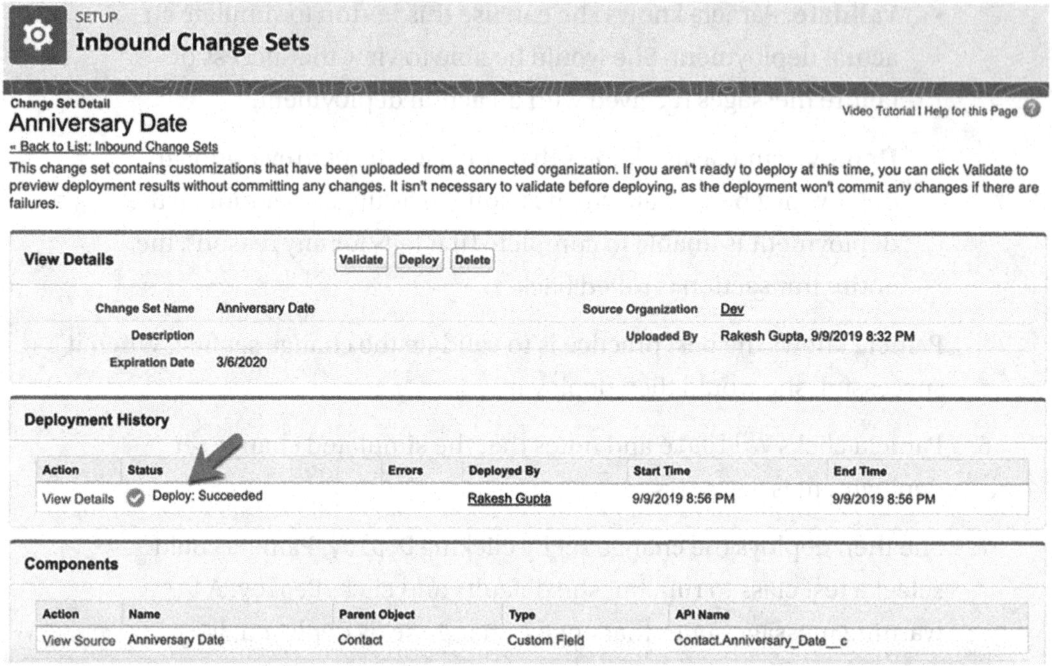

Figure 7-13. *Deployment successful*

If the status of the change set is Deploy: Succeeded, the change set was deployed successfully.

Benefits of Using Change Sets

There are numerous advantages to using change sets for deployment.

- There is a nice and tidy user interface to select changes that need to be deployed.

- Change sets can be validated before deployment.

- There is no need to install any other app to use change sets.

- It is easy to clone a change set.

- You can upload the same outbound change sets to multiple sandboxes or directly to a production org.

- Change set deployment is tracked with an audit trail!

Deploy Using Packages

Packages are containers that hold metadata components—either one component or a group of components. Packages are mainly used to distribute the app's metadata components that are not connected to the org. For example, you can use packages to deploy metadata components from a free developer edition org to one of your sandboxes or between two production orgs.

The best example of a package is an app from Salesforce AppExchange. There are two types of packages, as shown in Table 7-2.

Table 7-2. *Types of Packages*

Unmanaged Packages	Managed Packages
You can view and modify Apex code and other components included in an unmanaged package.	It is not possible to view the code of components, such as Apex class or Apex trigger.
Components can be edited in the organization after installation.	Components cannot be edited in the organization after installation.
The source organization has no control over the package after it is installed in a customer's org. Indeed, code within the package can be altered.	The code can only be altered in the source organization, where the package components were developed.
Unmanaged packages are generally used for module distribution among developers or freelancers.	Managed packages are generally used by Salesforce AppExchange partners to distribute apps to their customers.

The third type of package is called *unpackaged*. It refers to the components that exist natively in your organization, such as standard objects. Standard objects can go in an unpackaged package.

Points to Remember

- Email deliverability for new and refreshed sandboxes must be set to system email only.

- You can create and manage sandboxes from the production org.

- In a full sandbox, record IDs are identical to the production org's.

- You can't use change sets to delete or rename components.

- When deploying using a change set, the system runs all tests of Apex code. If your overall coverage is less than 75%, you are not able to deploy a change set.

- Change set deployment is tracked by an audit trail, which means you can check which components were deployed and when.

- Use packages when you want to distribute your metadata components to customers across the globe.

- To deploy metadata components through any tool requires system administrator permission.

Hands-on Exercises

The following exercises give you more practice with the platform, which ultimately will help you gain mastery of it and assist you in preparing for the certification examination. Remember, these are hands-on exercises, and you can find the answers in the appendix, but try to implement them in your Salesforce org, which is the primary goal of doing them. But try to do the exercises without looking at the answers!

1. It is possible to modify a trigger directly in a production org.

    a. True

    b. False

2. Which deployment tool activity is tracked by an audit trail?

    a. Change set

    b. Force.com IDE

    c. Package

    d. Force.com Workbench

3. Dennis Williams, a system administrator at GoC, created an application in his free developer org. Now, he wants to share the application with his peers so they can use the application without seeing any code and can provide their feedback. Which of the following deployment strategies should Dennis use?

   a. Change sets

   b. Managed packages

   c. Unmanaged packages

   d. SFDX

4. Dennis needs to create a sandbox that brings all lead records from production. GoC currently has 25,000 leads. Which sandbox should Dennis use?

   a. Developer

   b. Developer pro

   c. Partial copy

   d. Full

5. Dennis needs to create a sandbox for regression testing. GoC just completed an integration with one of the leading banks in the United States and is planning to start integration testing, which may create millions of records. Which of the following sandboxes should Dennis use?

   a. Developer

   b. Developer pro

   c. Partial copy

   d. Full

Summary

This chapter looked at the limits of declarative development vs. programmatic development. It also went through the application development life cycle, studied different sandbox types, and examined the deployment process in Salesforce by using an example.

Chapter 8 looks at the social and reporting capabilities of the Salesforce platform.

CHAPTER 8

The Power of Social Analytics

Abstract

Chapter 7 covered the limits of declarative customization, studied when to use programmatic development, explored various types of sandboxes, and discussed different deployment tools in Salesforce using a few real-life examples.

This chapter walks through the capabilities of reports and report types and examines the role dashboards play in rendering underlying analytics.

Introduction to Reports

Reports are a way to analyze how efficient teams are performing over time. For example, GoC's senior sales director, Richard Adams, wants to know the effectiveness of a campaign that ran during the current fiscal year. The campaign's report showed the current status of leads that came via referral.

Reports always generate data in real time based on the criteria you define. Reports respect an organization's security and settings. As a result, users only see records in the reports to which they have access.

To share reports with users, save them in a folder. Then, share folder access with the users. It is possible to create reports for standard and custom objects.

When you create reports in Salesforce, you must select a report type. A report type is nothing but a holding tank for records from one or multiple objects.

Report Types

Report types come in two flavors: standard and custom.

Standard Report Type

By default, standard report types are available for building reports on standard and custom objects, as well as *their* related objects. When a system administrator creates a new custom field, the field is automatically added to standard report types.

Custom Report Type

A custom report type allows you to build your own dataset or container. Users can select a report type in the report wizard to create a report. Remember the following key concepts when creating custom report types.

- You are allowed to select combinations of up to four related objects.

- You can select an object's fields (parent to child) and use them as columns in a report.

Setting up a Custom Report Type

Salesforce provides a simple wizard to create custom report types. Let's rejoin Pamela. Her manager wants her to create a report that lists all accounts that have at least one contact record, and each contact record must have at least one related opportunity associated with it. Pamela performs the following steps to create a custom report type.

1. She navigates to Setup (gear icon) ➤ Setup Home ➤ Feature Settings ➤ Analytics ➤ Report & Dashboards ➤ Report Types.

2. She clicks the New Custom Report Types button, which opens a window where she enters the following details.

   - **Primary Object**: Pamela selects the primary object from all the objects available in her organization, even those she doesn't have permission to view! In this case, she selects the Account object.

- **Report Type Label**: She enters a meaningful name for the report type label: Accounts with Contact and Opportunity.

- **Report Type Name**: This field is autopopulated based on the report type label.

- **Description**: Pamela writes some meaningful text so other developers and administrators can understand easily why this custom report type was created in the first place.

- **Store in Category**: She select the Account & Contacts category to store her custom report type.

- **Deployment Status**: Pamela selects Deployed.

Her screen looks like Figure 8-1.

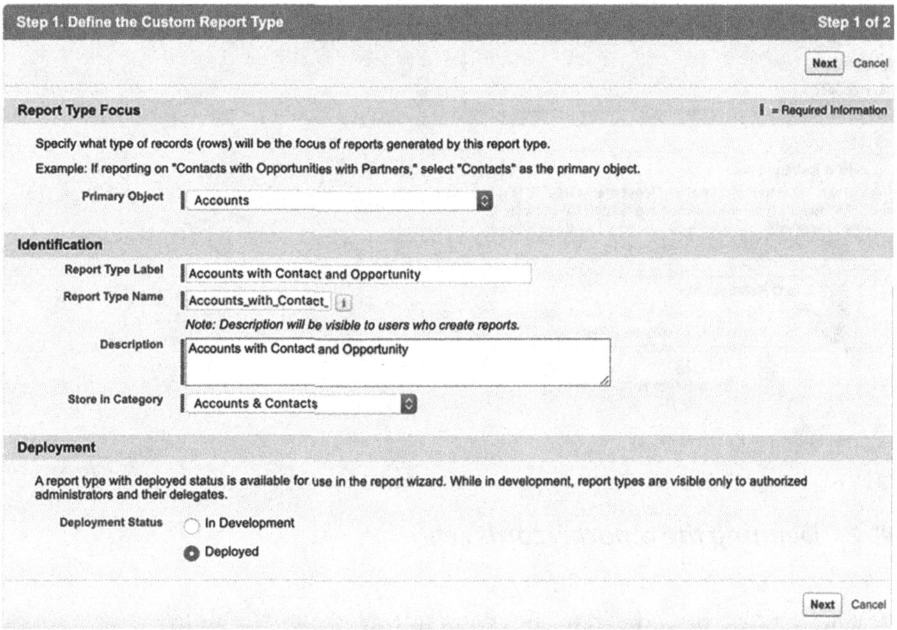

Figure 8-1. *Defining the custom report type*

3. When done, Pamela clicks the Next button.

4. With Account as her primary object, she now needs to relate another object to it. She selects Contacts as her secondary object and then selects the "Each "A" record must have at least one related "B" record." check box. She then selects Opportunities as the tertiary object and selects the "Each "B" record must have at least one related "C" record." check box, as shown in Figure 8-2.

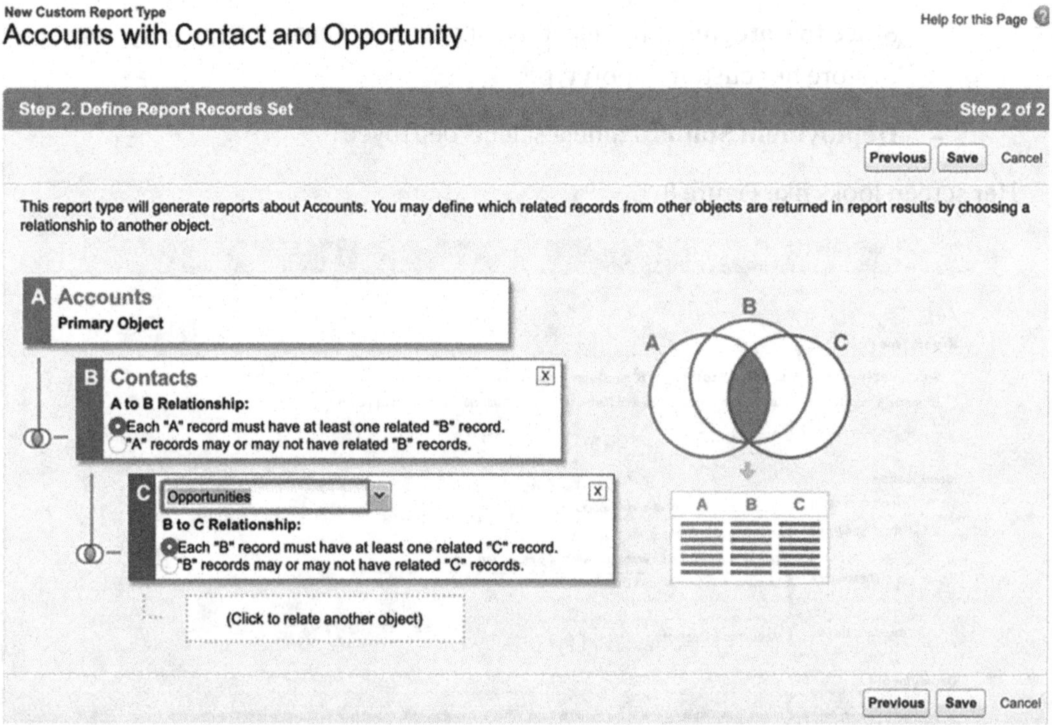

Figure 8-2. Defining the report records set

5. When done, Pamela clicks the Save button.

Report Format Types

Salesforce allows you to generate reports and assign them a format based on your business's requirements. Salesforce has four different report formats.

- Tabular

- Summary

- Matrix

- Joined

Tabular Report Format

Use the tabular report format to display rows of records in a table without any subtotal.

Pamela's task hasn't changed: create a report that lists all accounts with at least one Contact record, and each Contact record must have at least one related Opportunity record.

Pamela performs the following steps to create a custom tabular report.

1. She navigates to the Reports tab and clicks the New Report button.

2. She is redirected to a page where she must choose a report type. Pamela selects the Accounts with Contact and Opportunity report type, as shown in Figure 8-3.

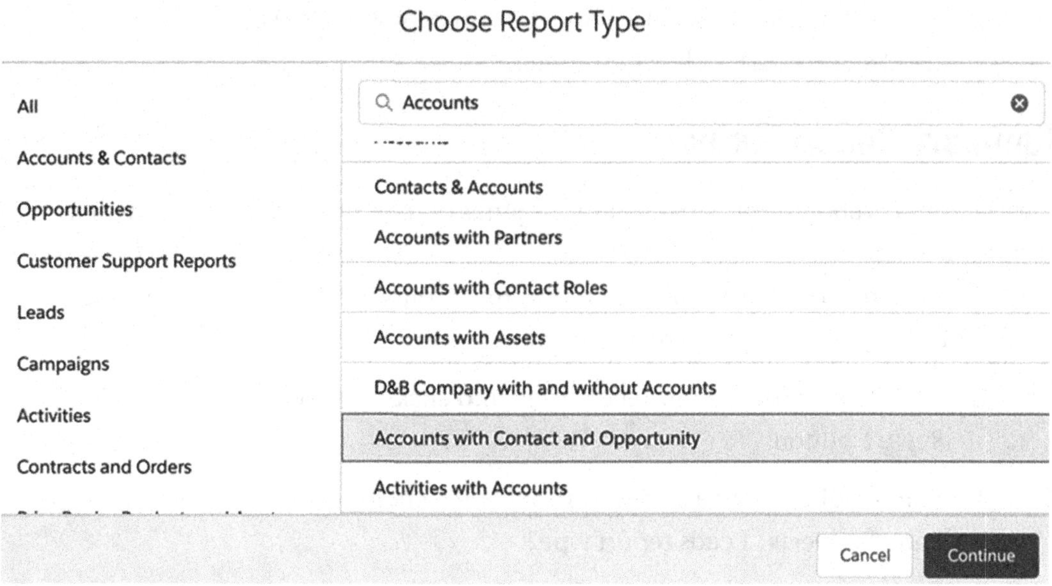

Choose Report Type

All	Q Accounts ⊗
Accounts & Contacts	
Opportunities	Contacts & Accounts
	Accounts with Partners
Customer Support Reports	Accounts with Contact Roles
Leads	Accounts with Assets
Campaigns	D&B Company with and without Accounts
Activities	Accounts with Contact and Opportunity
Contracts and Orders	Activities with Accounts

Cancel   Continue

Figure 8-3. *Choosing a report type*

3. When done, she clicks the Continue button.

4. In the next screen, she adjusts the filter by changing the Date field filter by selecting Created Date with the range All Time (see Figure 8-4).

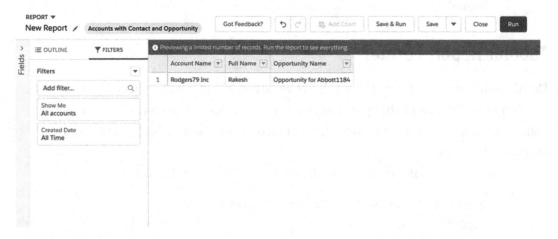

Figure 8-4. *Custom report*

5. When done, she clicks the Save button.

6. Finally, Pamela saves the report to an appropriate folder and checks the report folder sharing settings.

Summary Report Format

Use a summary report format to display groupings of rows of data. Let's start with a business use case.

Pamela needs to create a summary report that groups lead by lead source. She performs the following steps to create a custom report.

1. Pamela navigates to the Reports tab and clicks the New Report button.

2. She is redirected to a page where she must choose a report type. Pamela selects "Leads report type".

3. To apply row grouping based on lead source, she clicks the Lead Source drop-down, then Group Rows by This Field, as shown in Figure 8-5(numbers 1 and 2, respectively).

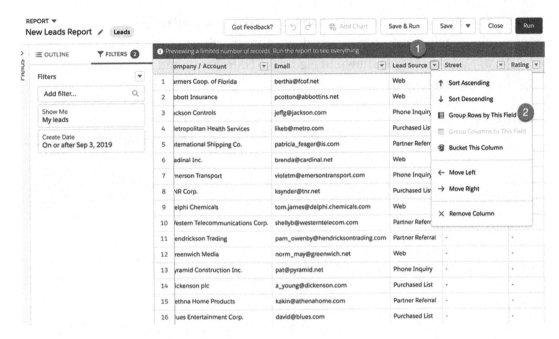

Figure 8-5. *Grouping by a field*

4. When done, she clicks the Save button.

5. She names the report "Leads grouped by source" and saves it in the Unfiled Public Reports folder.

6. When done, she clicks the Save button.

Matrix Report Format

The matrix report is the most complex report format. Use this report to summarize data in a grid. You can group records by both columns and rows. Let's start with a business use case.

Previously, Pamela created the "Leads grouped by source" report. Now, she must also display who owns these Lead records in the report. Pamela performs the following steps to create a matrix report.

1. Pamela navigates to the Reports tab and clicks "Leads grouped by source". Then, she clicks the Edit button.

2. She then applies column grouping based on the lead owner by clicking the Lead Owner drop-down and selecting Group Columns by This Field, as shown in Figure 8-6 (numbers 1 and 2, respectively).

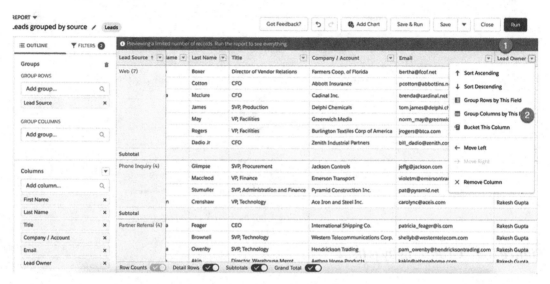

Figure 8-6. *Grouping by a field*

3. When done, she clicks the Save button.

Now, the report automatically changes the format from summary to matrix (see Figure 8-7).

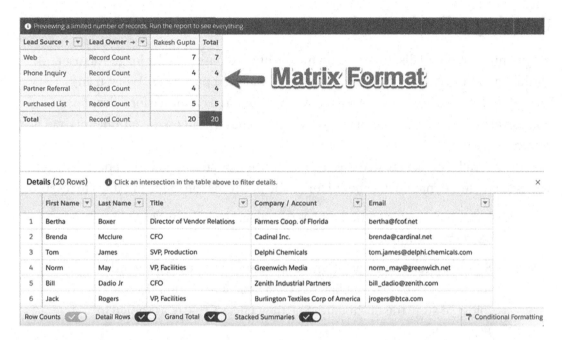

Figure 8-7. Matrix report

4.   Pamela clicks the Detail Rows toggle to hide report details.

Joined Report Format

Use the joined report format to combine multiple views of related information in a single report. For example, you may want to display a comparison between sales data from the current quarter of this year and data from the last fiscal year.

Dashboard Components and Its Types

The dashboard is a graphical representation of a report. It shows data from the source report graphically as a metric chart, gauge, donut chart, and so on, and it is created using Visualforce. Dashboard components provide a preview of your organization's key metrics and performance meters.

Business users can see all the details on a dashboard, regardless of the type of access they have to the records. But, as soon as they drill down to reports, users only see the records to which they have access.

Creating a Dashboard

A dynamic dashboard displays data on the dashboard based on the logged-in user. Dashboards can be created from summary and matrix reports only. When using Lightning Experience, you can even use a joined report as a source for a dashboard. You can also use a tabular report as a source if you put a limit on the number of rows it returns. Let's revisit Pamela.

If you recall, Pamela created the "Leads grouped by source" matrix report. Now, she wants to create a dynamic dashboard for it. She performs the following steps to do so.

1. Pamela navigates to the Dashboards tab and clicks the New Dashboard button.

2. She is redirected to a page where she must enter the dashboard name. In this case, Pamela types **Lead Dashboard** and selects a folder to store the dashboard. She then clicks Create, as shown in Figure 8-8.

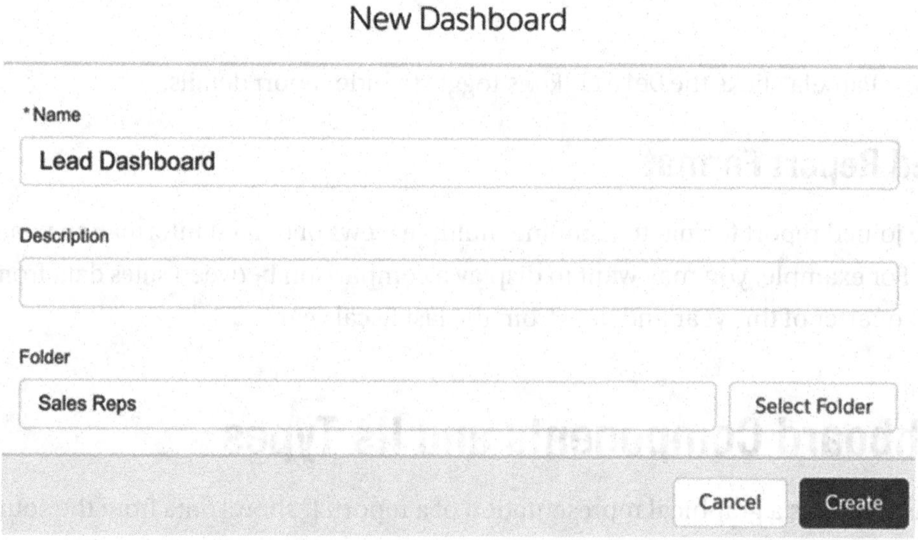

New Dashboard

*Name

Lead Dashboard

Description

Folder

Sales Reps   Select Folder

Cancel   Create

Figure 8-8. Creating a new dashboard

3. Next, Pamela clicks + Component to insert a component onto the dashboard.

4. She receives a prompt to select the report, so she selects "Leads group by source", as shown in Figure 8-9.

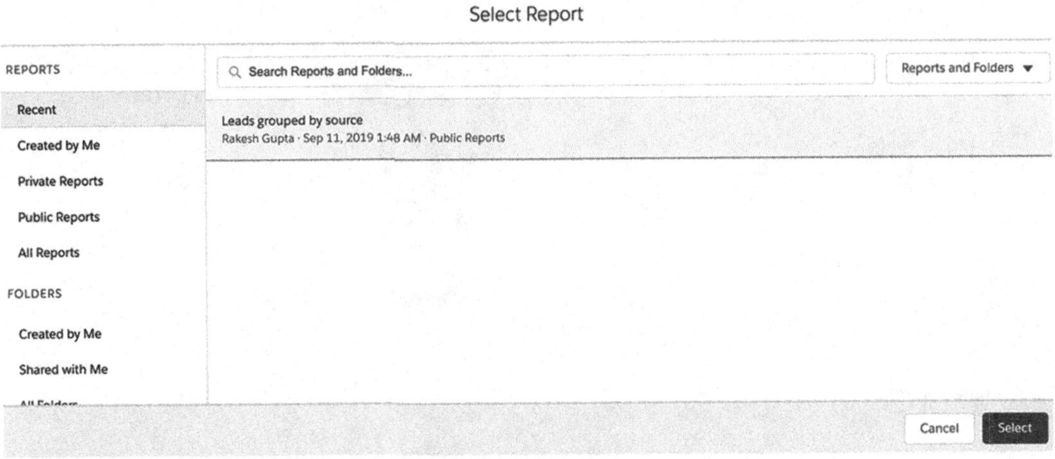

Figure 8-9. *Selecting a report*

5. When done, she clicks the Select button.

6. Next, she adds the component—in this case, she clicks the funnel chart icon—and configures it, as shown in Figure 8-10.

7. She can add multiple components to her dashboard. Each component shows data from one report. Pamela adds one more component—a donut chart—to her dashboard. She uses the drag-and-drop feature to reposition her components.

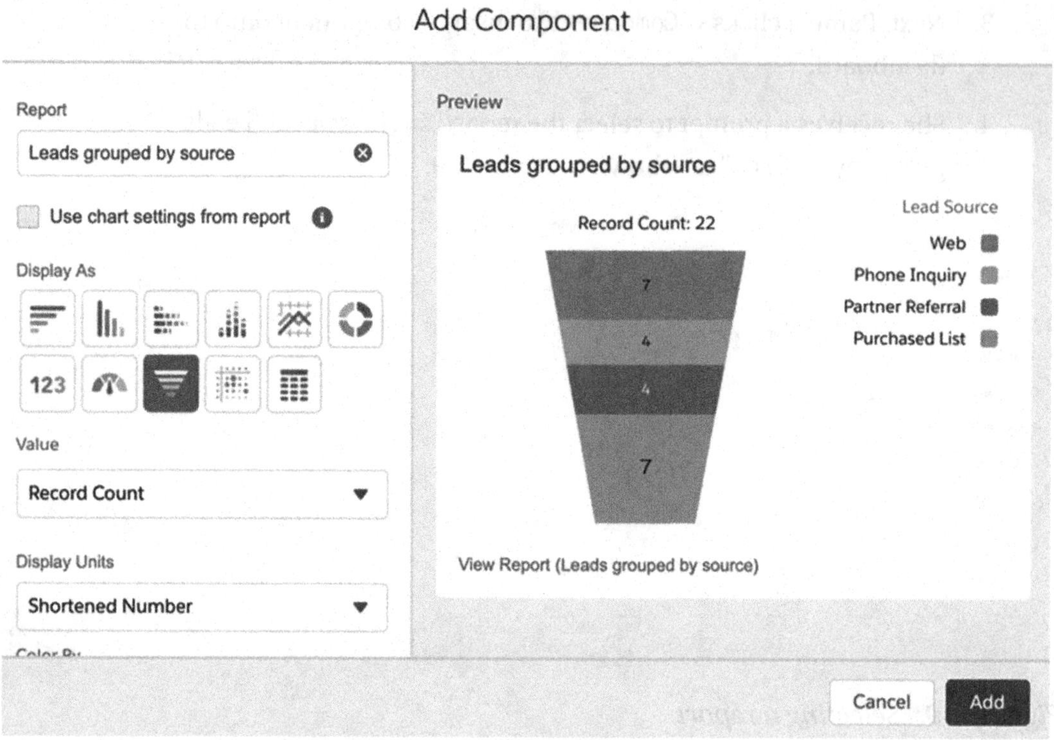

Figure 8-10. *Adding a component*

8.   When done, she clicks the Save button.

Making a Dashboard Dynamic

To make her dashboard dynamic, Pamela must go back to the dashboard she just created and perform the following steps.

1.   She navigates to the Dashboard tab and opens the Lead Dashboard.

2.   She clicks the Edit button.

3.   Next, she clicks Properties and goes to the View Dashboard As section. Salesforce offers three options.

a. **Me**: By using this setting, the dashboard runs as you. Everyone in the org sees the data on the dashboard per your access.

b. **Another person**: By using this setting, everyone in the org sees the same data on the dashboard.

c. **The dashboard viewer**: By using this setting, users see data based *only on their own access level*. If you select this option, you can't schedule the dashboard.

In this scenario, Pamela selects "The dashboard viewer" option, as shown in Figure 8-11.

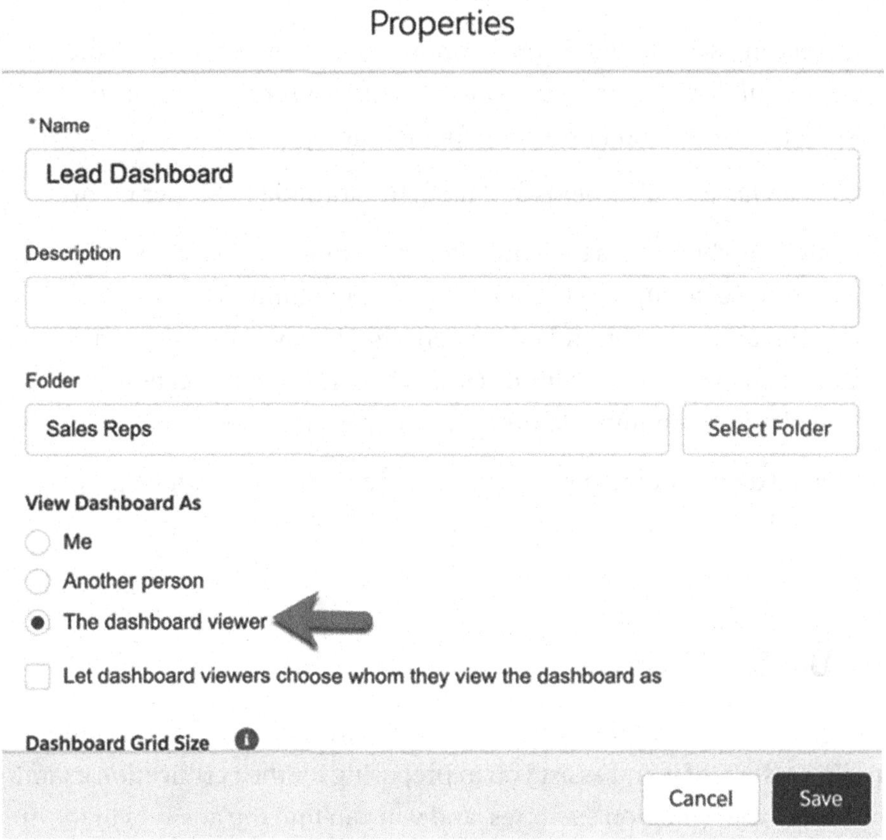

Figure 8-11. *Viewing the dashboard as*

4. When done, she clicks the Save button.

Points to Remember

- Your accounts, contacts, and leads aren't notified when you use Salesforce to view their social network profiles.

- Salesforce doesn't import or store your social information. Each time you select a social profile or a YouTube video, Salesforce retrieves the information you want to see directly from the social network in real time.

- System administrators or users who have Run Reports and Manage Dashboards permission can create dashboards.

- If you can't see the Add Formula option in the Fields section of the report builder, change your report format to summary, matrix, or joined. Formulas don't show up for tabular reports.

- You can have 20 filter fields and up to five formula fields per report.

- By default, the reports time out after ten minutes. You can contact Salesforce.com support to extend the timeout limit to 20 minutes for tabular, summary, and matrix reports. However, note that an extension of the timeout limit is not available for joined reports. Joined reports continue to time out every ten minutes.

- The maximum number of source report columns you can map to target fields is 100.

Hands-on Exercises

The following exercises give you more practice with the platform, which ultimately will help you gain mastery of it and assist you in preparing for the certification examination. Remember, these are hands-on exercises, and you can find the answers in the appendix, but try to implement them in your Salesforce org, which is the primary goal of doing them. But try to do the exercises without looking at the answers!

1. What are the components of the dashboard that use grand totals? Select two options.

    a. Metric

    b. Table

    c. Gauge

    d. Chart

2. Which report type is used to group rows of data and show their subtotals?

    a. Summary

    b. Matrix

    c. Tabular

    d. Detailed

3. Which report type is used to group rows and columns of data and show their subtotals?

    a. Summary

    b. Matrix

    c. Tabular

    d. Detailed

4. Dennis Williams, a system administrator at GoC, needs to create a report that shows leads created from social media as a source, their current stage, and who owns the lead. How would you instruct Dennis to do this?

5. Dennis must also show opportunities from the past and current fiscal year by the opportunity owner. How would you instruct Dennis to do this?

Summary

This chapter discussed the social features of Salesforce for accounts, contacts, and leads. It also went through the reporting concepts in Salesforce, including custom report types and different report formats, and examined the dashboard and dynamic dashboard concepts.

After reading this book, you should have gained a good understanding of Salesforce fundamentals and, as a result, should feel confident enough to take the Platform App Builder certification exam. Before you take the exam, make sure you complete the Trailmix at `https://trailhead.salesforce.com/users/strailhead/trailmixes/prepare-for-your-salesforce-platform-app-builder-credential`. Good luck!

APPENDIX

Answers to Hands-on Exercises

Chapter 1

1. b

2. b

3. c

Chapter 2

1. This is an exercise to explore the database architecture. There is no answer.

2. Use the `Date` field type. Refer to Chapter 2 to learn how to set up field-level security using Schema Builder.

3. Dennis should use the field types `Text (Encrypted)` and `Mask All Characters.`

4. Dennis should use the field type `Text Area (Rich).`

5. Dennis should use the field type `Geolocation.`

6. Dennis should select the field type `Formula` field. It will be resolved by the `Formula` field because this field is dynamic and always displays the current site value from the parent account.

7. This is a straightforward exercise. There is no "correct" answer.

8. Dennis should use the field type `Master Detail Relationship.`

R. Gupta, Salesforce Platform App Builder Certification Companion, Certification Study Companion Series

9. Advise Dennis to do the following:

    a. Select field type `Lookup Relationship`.

    b. Select the following options, while creating the `Lookup Relationship` field:

        •   Always require a value in this field in order to save a record.

        •   For `What to do if the lookup record is deleted?` select `Don't allow deletion of the lookup record that's part of a lookup relationship`.

10. This is a straightforward exercise. There is no "correct" answer.

11. This is a straightforward exercise. There is no "correct" answer.

Chapter 3

1. b

2. Set object OWD to Private; `Grant Access Using Hierarchies` = False.

3.

    a. Set OWD = Private; create a public group that includes the roles CEO, COO, Sales Rep-EMEA, Sales Rep-AMER, and the two users the from Sales Rep-APAC profile. Then, create sharing to grant Read Only access to the public group.

    b. Update the record owner to Pamela and make sure she has a role assigned.

    c. Via profile only, grant Read access on the `Address__c` object to all profiles.

4. Create a field `Social Security Number` with data type `Text (Encrypted)`, create a permission set to grant View Encrypted Data permission, and assign this permission set to the users mentioned.

5. c, because there are just ten records. We don't want to share all records owned by VP Sales.

6. The system administrator doesn't have a role assigned. If the system administrator—in this case, Dennis—has a role assigned, then he is below the CEO in the role hierarchy. Also, Dennis doesn't have Delete permission on the `Address__c` object.

7. The system administrator doesn't have a role assigned. If the system administrator—in this case, Dennis—has a role assigned, then he is below the CEO in the role hierarchy. Also, Dennis doesn't have Edit permission on the `Address__c` object.

8. Use Apex-managed sharing.

9. Set the Sales Rep-AMER profile `Lead` object access to Read, use a permission set and add Assign permission to it, and assign the permission set to the three Sales Rep-AMER users.

10. Use a permission set to add View All permission for the `Lead` object.

11. Use criteria-based sharing.

12. Set `Lead` OWD to Private, create a public group with all users except Rakesh and Munira, then write a sharing rule to grant Read access to the public group.

13. Set `Contact` OWD to be controlled by the parent.

14. Use Apex-managed sharing.

Chapter 4

1. This is straightforward.

2. Use a custom button or link.

3. Tell him to use component visibility features.

4. Tell him to use a quick action to update `Lead Status`.

5. This is straightforward. Include your findings about the Lightning app logo.

Chapter 5

1. Use lead support processes and record types.

2. Customize the Lead Lightning page and add its respective components.

3. Use lookup filters.

4. Use lookup filters.

5. Add a custom field.

6. Use lookup filters.

7.

    a. Use a validation rule.

    b. Use a custom permission in the validation rule and then assign it to users or profiles.

8. Use a formula field.

9. Use validation rules.

10. Use a rollup summary field.

Chapter 6

1. You have to use the Screen element to take the user input and display the outcome. But, to calculate the sum, you may have to use a formula.

2. Tell him to use an e-mail alert and Process Builder's immediate action Send Email.

3. Tell him to use Process Builder's immediate action Update Records to update the contact phone number.

4.

    a. Use the Post to Chatter action in Process Builder.

    b. Use the Update Records action in Process Builder.

    c. Use the Send Custom Notification action in Process Builder.

5. Tell him to use the Lightning Flow Create Records element and Process Builder to launch the flow.

Chapter 7

1. b

2. a

3. b

4. c

5. d

Chapter 8

1. a and c

2. a

3. b

4. Use a matrix report in which rows are grouped by stage and columns are grouped by owner.

5. Create a Summary report, with filter last and current fiscal year. Apply group by opportunity owner.

Index

A

AccountContactRelation, 38
Account object, 5, 38, 126, 184, 206
Apex-managed sharing, 75, 79, 223
Apex trigger, 75, 79, 135, 146, 165, 184, 201
API, *see* Application program
      interface (API)
AppExchange, 1, 17–18, 185, 201
   benefits, 19
   website, 18
App Launcher, 15–16, 94–96
Apple Inc., 2
Application governance, 187
Application life cycle, 186, 187
Application program interface (API), 9, 12,
      39, 151, 154, 158, 164, 186, 188
Approval process
   activation, 179
   approval steps, 177, 179
   creation
     approval page layout screen,
      172, 173
     automated approval routing, 171, 172
     details page, 174, 175
     email, 172
     information, 170
     initial submitters, 173, 174
     record editability properties,
      171, 172
     specify entry criteria, 170, 171
     steps, 170
   definition, 169
   final approval actions, 175, 176
   implementation, 169
   initial submission action, 176
   wizards, 169, 170
Automatic sharing recalculation, 79–81

B

Big objects, 6

C

Change sets, 193
   advantages, 200
   inbound, 198, 199
   outbound
     components, 195, 196
     creation, 194
     details, 194
     message, 197
     steps, 193
     target org, 197
     uploading, 196
Conga Composer, 18, 19, 21
Contact object, 5, 38, 49, 86, 140–142, 193
COUNT function, 129
CRM, *see* Customer relationship
      management (CRM)
CRM system, 1, 2
Cross-object formula, 125, 138
Custom buttons and links, 105–108

Customer relationship management
(CRM), 1, 2, 5, 8, 9, 11, 85
Custom fields, 28–30, 39, 45, 46, 128,
141–143, 170, 196, 206
Customization *vs.* programmatic
development, 186
Custom objects, 6, 7, 33, 34, 47, 51, 58, 62,
66–69, 71–73, 95, 125
Custom permissions, 83, 134–137
Custom report types, 206–208

D

Dashboard components, 213–217
Dashboard creation, 214–216
Dashboard dynamic making, 216–217
Data model, 27–28, 49
Declarative development
Apex trigger, 184
business requirement, 184
Closed Lost opportunities, 183
point-and-click tools, 183
potential customers, 186
Salesforce
APIs, 186
AppExchange apps, 185
create PDF, 184
Visualforce page, 185
validation rule, 184
Declarative *vs.* programmatic
development, 204
Defer Sharing Calculations, 80
Dynamic Lightning page creation
component visibility setting,
99–101
Lead object, 99
salesforce, 101

E

Einstein 1 Sales, 9, 12
Enterprise edition, 9, 12
Enterprise resource planning (ERP)
system, 6, 10
External data source, 37, 47
External lookup relationship, 33, 37
External objects, 6, 37, 47, 48, 125

F

Field dependencies, 41–45
Field-level security, 30–32, 85, 86
Formula fields
automation tools, 125
business needs, 124
definition, 124
list views, 127
Pamela Kline, steps, 125–127
standard/custom objects, 125
Free developer org, 188, 203

G

Global actions, 109
Global search, 17, 97–98
Governance limits, 21

H

Hierarchical relationship, 39, 122, 171
Home page, 96–97, 159–160

I

Indirect lookup relationship, 37–38
Integration Cloud, 2

J, K

Joined report format, 213
Junction object, 28, 38

L

Lead object, 5, 28, 42, 57, 60, 62, 75, 77, 79,
    82, 91, 99, 105, 110, 223
Lead Record Page (Sales), 102, 105
Lightning Connect, 47
Lightning Editions, 8, 11
Lightning Experience, 7
    App Launcher, 95, 96
    component-based design pattern, 94
    custom actions, 108, 109
    description, 93
    global search, 97, 98
    home page, 96, 97
    Lightning page (*see* Dynamic Lightning
        page creation)
    navigation menu, 94, 95
    page assignments, 102–108
Lightning page assignments
    custom buttons and links, 105, 107, 108
    parameters, 102
    visibility setting, 102–105
Lightning Platform, 20, 21
Lookup filter
    description, 122
    Pamela Kline, 122–124
Lookup relationship, 33, 34, 48
    vs. master-detail relationship, 36, 37

M

Manual sharing, 74–77
Manufacturing, 113–115, 119
Many-to-many relationship, 33, 38

Marketing Cloud, 2
Master-detail relationship, 36–37, 128
Matrix report, 211–213
MAX function, 129
Metadata, 24
    column labels, 25
    vs. data, 25
    need, 25, 26
    organization's data, 26
    Salesforce, 26
    table format, 24
MIN function, 129
Mortgage broker commission
        calculator, 152
    commission amount, 152, 153, 156–158
    screen element properties, 153, 154
    currency element properties, 155
    flow elements, connecting, 158
    flow version, activation, 159
    number element properties, 155
    Salesforce Flow Designer, 153
    Salesforce home page, 159, 160

N

Navigation menu, 15, 94, 95
Nest thermostat app, 17

O

Object-specific actions, 108
OData, 47
Opportunity object, 5, 49, 108, 109, 124,
        141, 142, 169, 170, 184
Organization-wide default (OWD)
    access for standard and custom
        objects, 58
    IKEA, 54, 56

Organization-wide default (OWD) (*cont.*)
   Pamela Kline, 54
   and role hierarchies (*see* Role
      hierarchies)
   security design model, 54
   types, OWD settings, 56, 57
OWD, *see* Organization-wide
     default (OWD)
Owner-based sharing, 74–75, 77–79

P, Q

Packages, 193, 201, 202
Pamela Kline, 7, 24, 54, 59, 62, 75, 83, 86,
      89, 122, 124, 125, 132, 146, 152,
      160, 183, 184, 190
Permission sets, 82, 83, 136, 222
   Apex class and Visualforce page
      access, 83
   app permissions, 83
   assigned apps, 83
   custom permission, 83
   field-level security, 85
   grant object access, 83–85
   object settings, 83
   service providers, 83
   system permissions, 83
   through profile, 86, 87
Picklist field, 48, 50
Profiles, 81
   custom, 81
   permission sets (*see* Permission sets)
   standard, 81
   system and object-specific permissions
     Modify All, 82
     Modify All Data, 82
     View All, 82
     View All Data, 81

Pro Suite edition, 9, 11
Public Read Only model, 54–58, 63, 68, 69,
     71, 74, 75, 79
Public Read/Write model, 55–58, 63, 72,
     73, 79, 87, 88

R

Read/Write access, 30, 75
Record accessibility, 74
Record sharing, 33, 59, 74–75, 81
Record types
   control Lightning record
      pages, 121–122
   description, 116
   page layout, 116–120
   purposes, 117
   Salesforce implementation, 113
Relationship types, Salesforce
   change field type, 45
   custom field, change field type, 46
   external lookup relationship, 37
   external objects, 47
   field dependencies, 41–43
   hierarchical relationship, 39
   indirect lookup relationship, 37, 38
   lookup, 33, 34
   lookup *vs.* master-detail
      relationship, 36, 37
   many-to-many relationship, 38
   master-detail, 36
   objects, 33
   select field type, 39, 40
   self-relationship, 35
   setup field dependencies, 43
Report formats
   joined, 213
   matrix report, 211–213

summary, 210–211

tabular, 209–210

Report types

custom, 206–208

standard, 206

Role hierarchies

CEO's role hierarchy, 64

GoC's organizational chart, 63, 64

hierarchies check box, 59

Pamela Kline

base-level setting, 60

campaign management, 62, 63

functional organizational structure, GoC, 59, 60

internal and external access, 61

requirements, 59

record access, 66–70, 72, 73

on record sharing, 59

Roll-up summary field, 37, 50, 128–131

S

Sales Cloud editions, 2, 8–10, 12

comparison, 8

core CRM objects, 8

Einstein 1 Sales, 9

Enterprise edition, 9

Pro Suite, 9

Starter Suite, 8

Unlimited edition, 9

Salesforce

big objects, 6

controlling data access, 55

customer customization, 23

customer data, 23

custom objects, 6

external objects, 6

multitenant architecture, 20

navigation menu, 15

OWD terminology, 55, 56

profiles (*see* Profiles)

Public Read Only model, 54

sign up for developer playground, 13, 14

standard objects, 5

standard *vs.* custom objects, 6, 7

stores data, 3

types of objects, 5

Salesforce Einstein AI, 13

Salesforce Flow, 182

actions, 145

advantages, 148

Apex trigger, 146

child records, updation, 165

Delete Records element, 167

Flow Designer, 167

Record Records element, 168

Record-Triggered flow, 165, 166

update records related to the opportunity record that triggered the flow option, 167

definition, 145

launching, 151

life cycle, 148

mortgage broker commission calculator (*see* Mortgage broker commission calculator)

Salesforce Flow Designer, 148–150, 153

series of screens, 145

triggered flow, 146, 147

unqualified leads, deletion

delete records element, 164

Flow Designer, 164

process flow diagram, 160, 161

record-triggered flow, 162, 163

steps, 161

triggered flow, 161

Salesforce Flow Designer, 148–150, 182

Salesforce Lightning Enterprise
      edition, 18, 27

Salesforce org, 187, 202

Salesforce platform
    Excel spreadsheets, columns
        and rows, 4
    objects and records, 4

Salesforce Trailblazer Community, 18

Salesforce user interface, 2, 3

Sandboxes, 187
    accessing, 192
    Apex class, 191
    creation, 190
    details, 190, 191
    developer sandbox, 189
    dev pro sandbox, 189
    field/metadata, 193
    full sandbox, 189
    partial sandbox, 189
    types, 188

Schema Builder, 26–28, 48
    advantages, 32
    create custom field, 28, 30
    field-level security, 30, 31
    field permission, 32

SDLC, *see* Software development life
      cycle (SDLC)

Self-relationship, 35

Service Cloud editions, 2, 8–10
    comparison, 11
    Einstein 1 Sales, 12
    Enterprise edition, 12

Pro Suite edition, 11
    support agents, 10
    Unlimited edition, 12

Sharing rules, 74
    Apex-managed sharing, 75
    criteria-based sharing, 74
    manual sharing, 74
    owner-based sharing, 74

Software development life cycle (SDLC),
    186, 187

Software development methodology, 186

Standard fields, 39, 48

Standard report types, 206

Starter Suite, 8

SUM function, 129

Summary report format, 210–211

T

Tabular report format, 209–210

U

Unlimited edition, 9, 12

V, W, X, Y, Z

Validation rules, 114
    annual revenue, 133, 134
    custom permissions, 134–138
    data evaluation, 132
    description, 131
    error messages, 132
    Pamela steps, 132